Butterfly
In The
Attic

My Story of Abuse and Abandonment
in Foster Care

by

Shandreka Monique Jones

Candy Publishing, LLC

© 2015 Shandreka M. Jones

Published by Candy Publishing, LLC

www.candypublishing.net

ISBN- 978-0692533871

Printed in the United States of America

Cover Art, Deborah Shedrick
www.dshedrick.com

Photograph Credits
Shandreka M. Jones

Butterfly In The Attic

Butterfly
In The Attic

DEDICATION

To all children who have been abused by those who
were supposed to protect them.

CONTENTS

INTRODUCTION

I can still feel the flames smoldering when I look back on my foster care days. It sounds strange and maybe a little crazy for me to say, but I don't regret anything that I endured during my years of abusive foster care. I keep telling myself that I survived for a reason. I often wonder *why* it happened to me, or should I say why it was *allowed* to happen to me. Whatever the reason is, I still harbor a lot of bitterness; I am *very* bitter.

I've forgiven my foster families with my mouth, but not my heart; my heart harbors a great deal of pain. I often wonder what I would do if I ran into any member of my foster families and what I would say. To be honest, I wonder what I would *do* to them more than what I would say to them. Hopefully, writing my pain will lead me to the path of fully forgiving those who were involved in my seemingly never-ending, abusive foster care experiences.

When I share my story with those close friends and family, they listen with open mouths and wide eyes because my story is, in fact, unbelievable. Now that I'm sharing my story publicly, I realize others may have similar horror stories of foster care, yet I don't discredit what I've been through. Each story is just as important and worthy of being told as the next. I wish enough of us would share our story to help shed some light on the system. Something has got to be done. The abuse must cease. Although we may share similar accounts, each of us has lived in our own personal hell. Without a doubt, no matter how gruesome my story is, I know there are plenty of foster care children out there who had it a lot worse than I did.

It's sad to say, but it's true. Some will live to tell their horror stories, but unfortunately others won't. Sadly, some foster children are still struggling to survive a life of abuse and neglect in their foster homes while others are struggling to live their lives *after* foster care. A normal childhood of fun and laughter is hardly the case for many children in the system. As a child, my normal was absolutely, one hundred percent abnormal.

The only reason I'm so eager to share my story is to become a voice for those in the foster care system. Not just a voice for those who are being mistreated, but I want to be a voice for those who have died in foster care, and even those who, as a result of being placed in abusive foster care homes, are now incarcerated, living on the streets prostituting, gang banging, and some are addicted to drugs.

It always seemed like a good idea to write a book, but secretly I didn't have the confidence to do it. In fact, I never felt smart enough to even hold an intelligent conversation. So writing a book was definitely out of the question. My grandmother and other foster parents planted deep in my brain that I was "stupid", "retarded", and "mentally retarded." I eventually believed those words. My grandmother constantly said, "You're going to be just like your bull dagger, drug addicted mother." Anything my grandmother could use to tear me down and apart, she used it to the best of her ability. That's one thing she was real good at.

I eventually had to stop thinking about my own inadequacies and considered all the children in foster care waiting for a voice to speak up and out for them. I knew they needed my story. The system needs my story. Future foster families need my story. I needed to tell my story not only for me, but to make a difference and hopefully bring about change in the lives of so many others in abusive foster care homes. My grandmother tried to keep me down, but I'm now stretching myself beyond her degrading words to uplift and encourage others. Writing this book was a challenge and I wanted to give up so many times, but I thought about my days in foster care and how I wished someone would have helped me.

One night, while driving home from one of my first semester graduate school classes, I began to reflect on how far God has brought me. I was an abused, neglected and lost child, yet I'd grown into a woman driving home to a loving family waiting for me to pull into the driveway. Not only was I enrolled in a great social work program at a reputable college, but it hit me that I had actually started writing my memoir.

After being told so many times that I would never amount to anything, I was finally doing something with my life that I was proud of. I gave up writing this book so many times and even doubted that I'd be able to finish college. I thought about how happy I was that I did not give up.

While reflecting, I turned the radio dial to listen to a station which played slow R & B music, and one of my favorite songs by Denise

Williams was coming through my car speakers. The song was *Black Butterfly*, and the lyrics captured my attention. Although I was driving on an open highway, I felt like I was in a trance and was magically turning into a beautiful butterfly.

I thought about the metamorphosis of a butterfly and how it was so similar to my life. I loved the line, "the ageless winds of time can catch your wings." By the end of the song, I was crying uncontrollably and thanking God for allowing me to survive my childhood of abuse. I thanked God that I realized I was now a beautiful butterfly that survived the cycles of life that had obviously been for my good. I pulled over, pulled out my galaxy note and immediately emailed my book coach, Kevin.

Kevin, I finally have a title for my book. I'm a butterfly.

The foster care system was designed to provide a safe place for children who have been voluntarily or involuntarily removed from their own home, which was either unsafe or maybe abusive. Other cases for required foster care could be the parents not being able to provide proper supervision for the children. The reasons are many, but regardless of what the reason is, foster homes are supposed to *foster* a safe, nurturing environment for children in need.

Unfortunately, that wasn't the case for me. From one foster home to another was more like one house of horror to another. With each move, I hoped to be placed in one of those safe and nurturing environments, but my hope failed me. This isn't the case for all foster care children, and I wish it had not been the case for me…but it was.

I didn't tell my story to point blame at agencies, I simply just wanted to tell *my* story. Not all foster families are bad. There are many foster families who go above and beyond to help a child in need, and there are many agencies out there working to place children in loving foster care homes to help them have a better quality of life.

I shared my story with Children's Rights, a national advocacy organization helping to raise awareness and inspire others. Children's Rights uses the law to protect thousands of abused and neglected kids when child welfare systems fail to do so.

*Children's Rights uses the law to hold governments accountable and defend thousands of kids when foster care systems fail. We have secured court orders mandating top-to-bottom child welfare reform in more than a dozen states. As a result, kids are safer. They get the education and health care they need. They have better foster homes. Best of all, children find permanent, loving families more quickly, ensuring they have the brightest possible futures. (www.childrensrights.org)

FOSTER FLASHBACKS

I traveled to Akron, Ohio in 1992 to attend my grandmother's funeral. It was supposed to be a trip to begin my grieving process, but on the day of her funeral, I felt absolutely nothing. I sat quietly - almost numb. When it was time to view the body, I remember nonchalantly walking up to her casket and looking down at her.

I couldn't even make fake tears to cry. I couldn't act sad because I wasn't. I didn't feel sorry for the cold, stiff, lifeless body of my grandmother. *Why should I?* She never cared for *my* body. The only thing she ever did for me was beat me, hit me, slap me, neglect me and degrade me with words that stripped me of every ounce of confidence and self esteem I had.

When I was just two weeks old, my mother dropped me off at this woman's house, and placed me in her care. What was supposed to be overnight care by my grandmother turned into seven years of a living hell with my mother's mentally disturbed and abusive mother, my grandmother.

Looking down at her, I thought, *Why are her glasses so thick?* Hmmm…maybe her glasses were so thick because she couldn't see how dirty I was. She never taught me how to bathe. Maybe she couldn't see how the sores in my head had gotten worse, and the rash on my body had spread. Maybe she couldn't see because she chose not to see the reality of the senseless abuse she inflicted upon me, and the reality of the evil spirit she had. Maybe she chose to be blind to the fact that I was her flesh and blood that she seemingly enjoyed beating.

I just walked away from her casket. I wasn't moved at all by the fact that my grandmother was dead. I didn't feel guilty for being so cold. Actually, I felt good because she showed me nothing except her cold heart the entire time I was with her. My abuse in foster care started with the dead corpse in the casket, Martha Ann Williams. I walked away and never looked back.

One may not consider a family member as official foster care, but it is – it's called kinship care. Kinship care is when a child is placed in the home of a relative or someone who knew the child before they were removed from their home. The family member who provides the care receives financial support from a foster care agency just as any other foster care family would. The benefit of kinship care is that a relationship has already been established between the child and the foster parent, and most kinship care is done without going through the court system. Yes, my grandmother was my first experience of foster care.

I said I never looked back after leaving my grandmother's funeral, but eventually I had to look back; I didn't have a choice. Not only did I have to look back over my life in general, but I had to look back over my many years in foster care. In order to be able to move forward in my life, I *had* to look back. I had to look back in order to begin a healing process; and that process is still incomplete. I had to look back in order to learn to deal with the constant triggers in my life that remind me of the abusive hands that were supposed to take care of me. Looking into my past helped me to understand my present.

If you were a stranger passing me on the streets, you might think I had it all together. I consider myself to be a beautiful, tall, plus-size woman with a nice smile and pleasant demeanor. I'm friendly and approachable. I have a God-fearing husband who loves me unconditionally, and I have a smart, handsome son who adores me in spite of my many imperfections. I seem to age well in spite of my past adversities and the many emotional and physical scars left on my body, which are many. On the outside, yes, I look as though I have it all together. I've learned if I keep myself looking good on the outside, I'll feel good on the inside.

Unfortunately, on the inside is a young girl who searched for love and acceptance most of her childhood only to be abandoned and ignored. It seems to be working pretty well for me to fake it until I make it. I *should* be the happiest woman alive, and for the most part I am happy, but those specially designed triggers have a mission to stir my dark past of the years I spent in foster care.

Sadly, the haunting triggers of my past continually come back to visit me. Sometimes the triggers come without warning, and I notice how they slowly creep up throughout my days and attempt to set up camp in my mind. There is never a day that goes by that I'm not silently battling to control my reactions to the uninvited triggers.

Some of those years of my dark past were spent with my own grandmother. I wish I could say my years with my grandmother were good years, but they were no different from my dark days spent in foster care. I would love to say my grandmother spoiled me with homemade chocolate chip cookies and milk and maybe some of my favorite meals, but she hardly fed me at all.

Sadly, I didn't have anyone to be a voice for me, or to pull me up out of my dark places until many years later when I decided to pull myself up. I once heard that God takes care of babies and fools. I always figured this was the reason why I was spared by His grace and mercy. The fact remains, I survived to tell my story.

I don't think my mother or grandmother had an ounce of maternal instinct; if they did, I didn't see it. I always thought a woman's maternal instinct would just kick in at some point, but my mother or grandmother never had a mother/child bond, so if they didn't receive it, I really couldn't expect them to give me the mother/child bond I desperately needed.

I'm just grateful that their lack of *supposedly* maternal instincts wasn't passed on to me. Moments after my son was born, and after the doctors removed the afterbirth and gave me some drugs, I was glued to my baby. To this day we have a mother/child bond that I love and cherish. I'm so thankful that I love my son because my chances of being like my mother and grandmother were high. I know God's angels were working overtime taking care of me, and they still are. I didn't stand a chance with my mother or my grandmother. Love wasn't a household word or action in our home. Again, God takes care of babies and fools.

Finally, in my early forties, I'm in a comfortable place in my life. It only took twenty- two years to have my "aha" moment, but I am grateful to experience it. I consider myself blessed and highly favored in spite of all I've gone through. I believe I was chosen for this journey way before my mother and father snuck behind Nana's house and conceived me. As I mentioned earlier, God has taken care of me ever since I was born, and he continues to take care of me - even when I feel like giving up.

I've come a long way, but I still have those days when I just want to stay in bed and not be bothered. It depends on the intensity of those triggers. A trigger can be something as simple as a stranger giving me directions using an authoritative voice. That voice can subconsciously snap me right back to how my grandmother and other foster parents would yell at me to get something done. Yes, it's that simple. I've gotten a lot better because I learned how to catch myself and coach my way back to reality. I've learned that everyone I come in contact with is not out to hurt me or deceive me, but I'm still very cautious. I don't think I will ever completely let my guard down. My guard, thus far, has kept negative people and things out of my life. Church folk call it God's gift of "discernment." Whatever it is, it's working, and I don't want to start changing things.

Finally, I've reached a point in my life where I'm able to do what I want to do, which is to go to school for my degree in Social Work and take care of my family. I'm finally able to breathe and maintain my peace of mind at a level where I can mentally function in school. I can learn something that will teach me how to help that specific population of the foster care system that seems to be ignored. This book is just the beginning of being a voice for those in need, and I'm determined to make some noise for them. Of course, it'll take more than just my voice to see change, but now is the time for me to sound off and be heard.

Although I have come to this new place in my life – a place of courage and increasing confidence, it is still very difficult to revisit my foster care pains, and even more difficult to write about them. Publicly sharing my story is also healing for myself as I've finally learned not to allow anyone to dictate how I should feel.

I realized that people who think they know how I feel or think they know what is best for me have not walked in my shoes; therefore, their opinion holds no value to me. I spent most of my life trying to please those who were supposed to protect me and love me. It didn't matter how good I tried to be or how pretty I tried to look, they still weren't happy with me. Even as an adult, for many years I was in the people pleasing business. I would buy my boyfriends and friends whatever money could buy.

I'd give 110% into the relationship and in return they would walk all over me and not be appreciative. I loved hard and I still do. I believe in the concept and meaning of love, yet because of my dark past, I've learned to give my love only to those who will love me back. I've also learned to love those who might not be able to love me back, but may need the example of love in their life in order to show it themselves. No, I'm not trying to save the world, but I have an obligation to love and share with those who are in my small corner of the world.

I also came to understand that keeping my story in a "private" status to protect my mother, father and others who played a part in my unfortunate childhood has only damaged me more. I guess it's in my nature to care about the feelings of others before I care about myself. I don't think putting others first is a bad thing, but sometimes I find myself suppressing my feelings to save or protect someone else. My mother told me she was proud of me for writing "my story." I really couldn't care less how anyone else felt, but having my mother's approval meant everything to me.

So this is my story and it's time for me to tell it. I am driven by my eagerness to help others heal who have also walked a painful foster care journey. I recall particular events that I can't seem to forget, and will probably never be able to forget. Each day I get a little better at coping with those triggers that surface way too often and insist on reminding me of my dark past.

Martha Ann Williams was her name, and she was a woman who suffered from a severe case of mental illness. She also had another name - grandmother. I found out my grandmother had a mental illness when I requested a history report from the Department of Social Services while researching my family history. She was diagnosed with mental illness when she was in her early thirties after giving birth to her son, my Uncle Gerald. She was also a diabetic, and required insulin injections twice a day.

With her fluctuating sugar levels and her bipolar disorder, her mood swings were volatile.

Martha Ann was a heavy-set woman, and she was very beautiful. She had curly shoulder-length hair, which she kept covered with her collection of wigs. When I attended her funeral, family members uncovered Martha Ann's real personality, but what I heard wasn't news to me. I had experienced her live and in color for myself. Usually, most funerals will say something good about the deceased person, but I don't remember anyone saying one single good word about my grandmother.

I heard comments like, "She was crazy and mean," "We felt so sorry for you when you stayed with your grandmother, but she wouldn't let us come next you," or "We were so afraid of her." My grandmother came from a large family. I'm not exactly sure how many siblings she had, but I know it was around twelve brothers and sisters, and this is based on what I heard. There are stories of my grandmother fighting her mother and sisters. It wasn't a little smack here and there, but more like throwing boiling hot water at each other. I had never heard anything like this before, but after living with my grandmother, I believe every word of it.

I'm not sure why they fought all the time. It could be the generational curse amongst the women that my Uncle Gerald talks about. I supposedly broke the curse because I gave birth to a boy. I felt like I cheated by breaking the curse, but the bottom line is that I broke it - period. So if having a son contributed to the broken curse, so be it. Martha Ann had two children, my Uncle Gerald and my mother Diane. According to my mother and Uncle Gerald, my grandmother was very abusive physically and emotionally. As crazy as it sounds, I was happy it wasn't just me that she was abusive to.

My grandmother showed nothing but hatred towards my mother. I guess she didn't know any better because of her mental illness, and I say this because nobody in their right mind would abuse a child the way my grandmother abused me. I was told that my grandmother actually loved my mother's father, who unfortunately was a married man.

Personally, I don't think she really loved him; but that's my opinion. When my mother's father found out that Martha Ann was pregnant, she never heard from him again. I think her ego was hurt because later my mother learned that my grandmother threatened her father to tell his wife about the affair if he didn't come back to her. The threats didn't work because he never came back for my grandmother or his child.

Martha Ann was embarrassed and hurt from being rejected. I believe she couldn't control him to do and be what she wanted, but she sure was consistent in trying. Her last husband, George, was like her puppet. She would tell him to jump, and he'd ask how high. She had complete control of him – just the way she liked it.

My grandmother dealt with the rejection from her love by taking her anger out on my mother. She would abuse her to the point of tying her to a bed and beating her almost to death. Eventually, my mom got tired of the abuse and ran away from home. My mother started running away at the age of nine. She couldn't take the abuse. *I know the feeling.* To this day, my mother has no idea who her father is, and she's hurt that she doesn't. She tells me all the time she would've been a perfect "daddy's girl" if she had the chance. It breaks my heart that she feels this way because I believe her - she would've been the ideal daddy's girl.

Uncle Gerald shared unspeakable things with me that my mother endured at the hands of her own mother. My grandmother would beat her until she got tired of beating her. *Who does this?* Then she would take a break and get right back to beating her. My uncle began running away from home at a young age, and the abuse towards my mother got worse. I can only imagine what this did to Uncle Gerald, but he was later placed in a group home.

To this day, my uncle swears that my grandmother would've killed my mother if she had stayed one day longer. He has shared his guilt for leaving my mother behind, but he didn't know how to help her. He was a child himself, and I'm sure full of fear of what he had to witness from his own mother. My uncle wanted his mother dead way before it was her time to go.

Uncle Gerald considered his sister, my mom, his best friend. I understand him not being able to stay around and watch his only sister be abused. He chose to run away because that's how his young mind told him to react. He felt helpless and hated his mother for the pain he inflicted on his sister, my mom. Uncle Gerald may not have endured as many severe beatings as my mother did, but he received his fair share.

Sometime during his middle teens, Uncle Gerald was locked up for dealing drugs and gang banging. It was unfortunate for him, but at the same time it might've been a blessing since it spared him from Martha Ann's cruelty and abuse. Abuse has the capability of breeding abuse, so being locked up may have saved Uncle Gerald from acting out even more. Uncle Gerald was used as my grandmother's personal boy slave because she didn't want him out of her sight. When she was on her menstrual cycle she would make my uncle wash out her reusable menstrual towels.

I'm so thankful my uncle shared this part of his life with me because it's also my life. That generational curse may have stopped with me, but I also endured my share of abuse – more than my share!

My mother claimed she walked in on my grandmother and Uncle Gerald while they were kissing, which resulted in my uncle eventually trying to kiss my mother, his sister. He was merely doing what he learned to do. My mother stabbed Uncle Gerald in the chest with a fork, but I don't think he was hurt badly. My mother didn't play. Although he was young, back in those days they weren't rushing children to the emergency room.

Looks aren't the only thing inherited in my family. Not only does my mother resemble her mother, she also inherited her mental illness. My mother was diagnosed with bipolar disorder when she was in her early forties. She accepted the treatment for it, but a few years after being diagnosed, she stopped her treatment and went back to her old ways, and everyone around her suffered the consequences. I guess she just got tired of taking her medication not thinking of what she was doing to herself and everyone else around her.

If Uncle Gerald's recollections are true, this generational curse of mental illness goes back as far as my great-grandmother. My uncle told me that my grandmother was physically and mentally abused by her mother. So this madness was part of a vicious cycle handed down from one generation to another.

The stories that I've heard about how my grandmother treated my mother are horrifying, and almost unbelievable. I've never been able to understand how someone can literally hate their child so much and be so cruel. When I consider the mental illness, I wonder if the women in my family had a choice about how they treated their own children – including me. Many times, after extended beatings, my grandmother left my mother for dead. I'm thankful my mother is alive.

Martha Ann's mental and physical abuse is what finally caused my mother to run away from home at the age of eleven. It wasn't long after running away that she became a ward of the state. After losing custody of my mother and after Uncle Gerald got locked up, my grandmother had no one to abuse…until I was born. After all the abuse my mother endured on her body and at such a young age, it's a miracle that she was able to conceive and carry me for nine months. I was delivered a healthy baby. Yes, God takes care of babies and fools… I'm a witness!

It wasn't until my young adult years that I thought about that generational curse of mental illness and began to wonder if I had a dose of that illness. While working towards my degree in Social Work, research has helped me to better understand the major part mental illness played in the lives of my mother and grandmother. Unbeknownst to me, my own mental well-being was under scrutiny. I've learned that mental illness in foster care children is no secret, and antidepressants usually come with the package. It doesn't surprise me because of what I've experienced first-hand.

Children who are involuntarily placed in foster care have already dealt with some type of traumatic or disturbing circumstance in the home, which resulted in them having to leave the home in the first place. God forbid the child is placed in another home, with hopes of being properly cared for and protected, only to walk right into an unfamiliar environment with some of the same or worse mistreatment, neglect or abuse. Children don't ask to come into this world, so they shouldn't be subject to living in anything less than a safe and loving environment. I don't think that's asking for too much.

My mother became pregnant with me while she was in foster care. She hid her pregnancy for as long as she could because her boyfriend's mother did not approve of her pregnancy and made it clear that my mother wasn't good enough for her son and never would be. She also went as far as calling my mother a slut and accused her of sleeping with multiple men. If that wasn't enough hatred from one woman, she even denied the fact that my mother and her son were even a couple. Well, technically they weren't a couple, but they were together long enough to conceive me. They both admitted they weren't in a committed relationship, but were together only for the sex. Ironically, my father had another woman pregnant in the same city, and planned to marry that woman. They even had a wedding date set.

My mother's boyfriend and his entire family turned against my mother. My mother was young, terrified and all alone, and I was right there with her – in her womb.

My mother's pregnancy was eventually exposed by her foster mother, Nana, an older woman who only took abandoned females into her home. Nana was a small, meek, older woman who tried to help anyone who was in need. Nana's number one priority was to teach young women how to be young ladies. My mother was seventeen years old when she birthed me and she wasn't in any mental or emotional condition to take care of a newborn baby, so she was placed in a foster home with other young girls like her - young girls who didn't have a clue about raising a child and probably didn't have anyone in their life to emulate a nurturing mother.

To my surprise, while looking into my family history, I found out that my mother's boyfriend was related to Nana, which is how he and my mother hooked up at their "family gatherings." It's funny how life revolves in a big circle because I ended up right back with the family that denied me over twenty years ago.

Nana's heart was for helping broken women in need; however, rumors reported that Nana's interest in young women went far beyond teaching them how to act like a lady. It was more like a ladies of the night environment. Nana took in abandoned teenaged females and would prostitute them out.

I've never shared this information with my mother because she would be disappointed, probably devastated. Nana was the only woman that showed my mother some love, so I wouldn't dare take that away from her. Sadly, Nana lost her eyesight due to diabetes in her early sixties. My mother told me Nana never worked because she had heart problems since she was a little girl.

I was born on June 16, 1973 in Mount Vernon, New York Hospital. I have to accept my date of birth because I have yet to see my original birth certificate. I trust my mother to know the day I was born. She told me I was a beautiful, eight-pound, nine-ounce baby with a head full of curly, black hair.

My mother didn't have many pictures of me, but she did have the first picture that was taken of me at Mount Vernon Hospital. Twenty years after I was born, I was able to see that one picture and confirm that I really was a beautiful baby. My mother and I were released from the hospital not long after my birth, and my stormy and uncertain journey began.

The following is an actual document from
Children's Services Adoption Unit NY

2.) <u>Health History of Birth Mother:</u> child victim of physical abuse and neglect, history of placement in foster care due to neglect and as Person in Need of Supervision (PINS) due to behavioral problems such as running away; unspecified mental illness of maternal parent, diabetes of maternal parent; health history of birth mother's paternal family not stated in record

3.) <u>Health History of Birth Father:</u> unknown

4.) <u>Facts and Circumstances Relating to the Nature and Cause of the Adoption:</u> Record reflects the biological mother has a history of foster care placement due to chronic abuse and neglect received from her mother. Her mother (the maternal grandmother) has a history of at least two psychiatric hospitalizations in early 1960's, with unspecified diagnosis. There is a history of significant physical and emotional abuse inflicted by maternal grandmother towards the biological mother. The biological mother's family consisted of maternal grandmother, step-father and brother. The step-father was reportedly dominated by his common-law-wife. He reportedly did not intervene to protect the children and the record indicates he later became an alcoholic. The biological mother's brother was placed to a juvenile facility as an adolescent due to various acts of delinquency at school and community. He too was reportedly abused in the home, but not as severly as his sister. He returned to the home of his mother and step-father as an adult. Record also mentions he became a drug addict as an adult.

The biological mother entered foster care at age 11. She was 16 years old and in foster care when she gave birth on 6/16/73 to a female child. There are no birth documents in the record in reference to the child. There is no recorded information or documentation in reference to the child's biological father.

When the child was 2 months old, the child and birth mother returned to the home of the maternal grandmother. Record indicates that the mother intended the maternal grandmother to provide care until she finished high school. According to the record the maternal grandmother kept the infant, but the biological mother was "turned away." The record also reflects the maternal grandmother refused to allow the biological mother any further contact or visits. The biological mother was in several different foster care settings, and often ran away from foster care. The infant child remained in the home of the maternal grandmother, however, there is no further recorded information about the child'd growth and development.

The next available record of contact was in May 1981, when there was a report to Child Protective Services. The child appeared in school with bruises, resulting in a report to Child Protective Services. The record indicates that an exam of the child's body revealed the following: "multiple welts on the right arm; bruises on inner right arm; a laceration on the inner right wrist; welts and bruises on outer left arm; an eight inch welt on the upper back with a laceration in the middle of the upper back; welts on her legs and scratches inside the nose; a contusion on the left forehead. All these marks appeared to be fresh. In addition there were five small scars on the child's neck and a scar at the corner of the right eye which appeared to be old." The record indicates the child reported being "beaten" by maternal grandmother with a "cord", and also reported grandmother "hitting her face against the kitchen table" and grandmother "banging her head against the wall." Record indicates child also "stated that her grandmother frequently beats her." Child was immediately placed into foster care for safety and protection.

The biological mother came forward and cooperated with CPS, however, the record states she felt she was "unable to take on the responsibility" of caring for her daughter, who was now 8 years old and had not been living with her since age 2 months. The family court determined that the maternal grandmother did not have legal custody of the child, therefore a Voluntary Placement Agreement was signed by the biological mother. The child remained in a foster home with the goal of return to the biological mother. The biological mother was to obtain suitable housing and establish a relationship with her daughter through regular visitation. The record indicates that the biological mother was able to plan for her daughter's return and showed this by maintaining visits, attending therapy and securing housing. In August 1982, child was returned to the biological mother's care.

In January 1983, the child returned to foster care due to being left alone upsupervised by her mother. Mother admitted to leaving the child home alone and stated she frequently left the child unsupervised. She also threatened to "beat" the child and threatened to "kill" the child, however, there was no record of physical abuse. The record indicates that the child called the police to report herself being alone. It is stated that the maternal grandmother told the child to call the police. CPS and the police were concerned by the biological mother's emotional reaction, as well as to her admission to leaving the child unsupervised regularly. A Neglect petition was filed with family court and the child was returned to the same foster home in which she previously resided. The record states child had "attachments to her former foster parent" and foster parent "readily accepted" child back into her home. The Court adjudicated the child neglected by biological mother and approved foster care placement. The court also ordered that the "child shall not be placed with the maternal grandmother under any conditions."

Child remained in that foster home, however several issues emerged. The child had an "infection," possibly "ring worm," on her scalp and the foster mother was referred to a doctor. The doctor wrote a presciption for "an antibiotic, a crème and a medicated shampoo." Foster mother was directed to shampoo the child' s hair daily and "leave the hair loose, not braided."

In a follow up doctor's appointment, it was determined that medical treatment was not provided as directed, since the child had her hair in braids, her hair had not been washed daily, and the condition of the scalp continued. A report was made to Child Protective Services with allegation of "lack of medical care." It could not be determined from the record if that report was indicated or unfounded, however, there were other issues of concern in the foster home: the child did not seem to be adjusting well, her grades and behavior in school were extreemly poor; foster parents were unsure of their ability to meet her emotional needs; the maternal grandmother made unwanted phone calls to the home; there was concern about child's expression of sexualized behavior, for example walking into the foster son's room naked; and foster mother felt the biological mother's feelings of resentment towards her interferred with the mother's ability to plan for the child.

Therefore, DSS made a decsion to transfer the child to another foster home. In September 1983, child transferred to a new foster home, which eventually became the child's adoptive home.

Since the child's removal in 1983, the biological mother was inconsistent in her ability to maintain contact with the Department of Social Services. She often failed to attend visits or be available to plan visits. She had difficulty addressing her daughter's emotional needs, which was attributed to the fact that "she herself was abused brutally by her own mother." In 1985, the mother signed a voluntary surrender of her parental rights to allow her child to be adopted by the foster parents. Mother also admitted to "making up" the name of the child's father for purposes of public assistance; she said she did not know anyone by that name.

5.) <u>Available Birth History:</u> no birth record available

6.) <u>SIBLINGS:</u>   Gender: Female -   Age(s):
     ☒ NONE   Male –   Age(s):

GRANDMA DEAREST

My account of those early times on my stormy journey came from stories told by my grandmother, mother, Uncle Gerald, and from what I could piece together from my sketchy memory. It bothers me that my memory is vague, but at the same time I believe God has protected me by not allowing me to remember all the details of my depressing past. Uncle Gerald once told me to stop digging in my past because I would open Pandora's box. *I'm not sure what that means.* Although I'm pretty sure I had some good times, I try to avoid the "back in the day" conversations. My bad memoires outweigh my good memories, but it is what it is.

Nana helped my mother take care of me because at seventeen years old my mother's parenting skills were non-existent. When I was a few weeks old, my mother found me in bed not breathing. She grabbed me, and she and Nana jumped in the car to take me to the hospital. With Nana speeding through the streets of Mount Vernon, she instructed my mother to stick my head out the car window. My mother says I immediately started to breathe again. I always wonder if I would be alive today if Nana had not been there to help. I also wonder if my mother's motherly instincts would've kicked in had she been alone. Either way, I know that because my life was spared, God has a purpose for my life. That incident was the first time I had a near-death experience, but it certainly was not the last.

Although my mother and grandmother's relationship was estranged, my mother desperately craved her mother's love and approval. To this day she speaks openly about how she wished her mother loved her. She hoped that my birth would bring some peace to their relationship. My mother also prayed that her mother wouldn't hate me as much as she hated her – her own daughter. It wasn't long after one of my mother's visits to her mother's home that proved they would not have the mother / daughter relationship she longed for.

One day, my mother left me with my grandmother so she could go hang out with her friends. Little did my mother know that that would be the last time she would see me again because Martha Ann kept me. Uncle Gerald told me some years later that Martha Ann never had any intention of giving me back. I often wonder if my hell was premeditated. You never know what goes on in another person's mind. Martha Ann accused my mother of neglecting me because I had a bad rash, from soiled diapers, that covered my whole body. Is this true? I'll probably never know, but I do know that the day I was dropped off at my grandmother's is the day I went straight from the frying pan into the fire.

I lived with my grandmother on the fifth floor of her one-bedroom apartment in a nice neighborhood in Yonkers. The neighborhood was pretty quiet considering it was in an area that never slept. The dining room was my room. I slept on a pull-away bed with the mattress fully covered with plastic. I guess the plastic was so my grandmother could protect her investment; everything she owned was protected by plastic. She covered all her couches, lamp-shades and kitchen chairs. She even ran a plastic runner from the front door all throughout the apartment.

At that time, my grandmother was married to a very timid man. He wasn't my mother's or my uncle's father. My grandmother didn't give either of her children the satisfaction of knowing who their father was.

Her husband never said much; he just drank alcohol and smoked cigarettes. He smelled like a walking ashtray and his breath smelled like alcohol, garlic and raw onions all mixed together. I remember him having a horrible cough that sounded like he was coughing up a lung. He was a skinny, dark-skinned man with a cocked eyed. That cocked eye didn't frighten me. To be honest, I didn't even realize it was abnormal. George was his name and he was kind to me. He felt sorry for me and on multiple occasions he jumped in to try to save me from my grandmother's horrendous beatings. He was never successful at saving me, but I was always thankful for his attempt.

My grandmother didn't have many friends to visit her, which might've been a good thing due to her filthiness. As if she needed an animal along with her filthiness, she had a poodle named Gomet Star. The poor poodle's gray fur was matted and black with filth. I don't think my grandmother took him out much because he handled most of his business in the house - in his corner. I know for a fact that my grandmother didn't clean up after him, so I'm pretty sure her timid husband did. Her husband pretty much did everything in the house, but it was still filthy. The traditional gender roles were switched in this household; my grandmother wore the pants. At times, the odor in her house was unbearable, but the normal stench didn't take long to get used to it. I thought it was normal.

Although we lived in a decent apartment building, the roaches and rats were uncontrollable in Martha Ann's apartment, and she didn't seem to care. She would step on the nasty bugs and rodents and keep moving. It didn't seem to bother her one bit. I had never seen anything like this before. Between my grandmother's soiled panties hanging in the bathroom, used syringes all over the place, my timid grandfather's stale cigarette smoke, the smell of alcohol that permeated the walls and furniture, and the dog shit in the corner, our home looked and smelled pretty much like an outhouse.

We weren't very sanitary. I say "we" because she never taught me how to care for myself. I lived what I learned. I don't remember taking many baths or practicing anything close to good hygiene. My grandmother would hide her body odor with her perfume. It wasn't until many years later when I joined the military that I learned how to take care of my body.

As a teenager, the most I did was wear deodorant. I don't think I ever owned a toothbrush or a brush for my hair. Today, my bathroom overflows with toiletries. I can't seem to get enough of the sweet smells and how they make my body feel when I use them. Each morning and night, I take extra time to take care of my body. It seems like I have a product to cover every body part with. I'm not ashamed to say that I treat myself to some high quality products that aren't sold at the corner store, but like I said...I treat myself. Sometimes I feel like I'm making up for the times when nobody taught me how to care for myself. My grandmother sure didn't take the time to teach me.

My grandmother was a very unstable woman. She was evil and seemed to hate everyone, including me. I don't know why, maybe because I am my mother's child. I remember from a very early age that she didn't care for me much by the way she treated me and how she talked to me. Actually, she never talked to me; she always talked at me. Even as a young child, I felt like I was a burden to my own grandmother. She acted like she didn't want me, but for some reason she didn't want anybody else to have me - not even my own mother, her daughter. None of it made any sense to me then, and it still doesn't.

My mother was furious that Martha Ann stole me from her. Uncle Gerald, who was out of jail at the time, witnessed Martha Ann and my mother fighting over me every time they ran into each other in public. My mother told me she came for me many times but Martha Ann wouldn't let her in the apartment. I'm not saying that didn't happen; I just don't remember. If what my mother says is true, I guess she stopped fighting for me because I ended up staying with Martha Ann.

My mother either had to stop fighting for me, or my grandmother threatened her and put the fear of God in her to stop trying to get me back. No child wants to believe their own mother didn't fight for them or didn't care enough about them to keep them, but it happens more times than we care to believe. Nevertheless, this is how a lot of children end up in foster care homes.

I was the only child in my grandmother's house, which left me feeling very lonely. Having my bed in the dining room made me feel extra lonely, especially at night when it was time for bed. There were no walls with pictures on them to look at, no dolls on my bed, no dresser or chest of drawers full of clothes or topped with my favorite things to look at. I didn't even have a door to shut to keep the monsters away. I only had my imaginary friends and my poodle Gomet Star for company.

I trusted my imaginary friends. When I was lonely, which was most of the time, they made feel as though I belonged. They made me feel loved and wanted. They allowed me to talk about anything I wanted to talk about, and in return they told me anything I wanted to hear. My dark nights weren't so dark after my long beatings because my imaginary friends would console me until I fell asleep. They quietly listened to me sniffle and they never told me to shut up or be quiet. They wiped my tears away and gave me a comfort I believe every child deserves, whether in foster care or not.

I can't remember if I gave my imaginary friends names or not, but they always called *me* by my name. I remember them telling me, "Don't worry, Monique, we'll be okay" or "Don't cry, Grandma loves you. That's why she beats you." I believed my imaginary friends; I always did. They didn't have a reason to lie to me.

As a child, my grandmother confused me and made it hard for me to process her treatment towards me. Hate is a strong word, but I believed with all of my abused and broken heart that Martha Ann hated me. The confusing part is when she did things for me that made me *think* she loved me. She would dress me in the nicest clothes and she kept plenty of toys around. She also put me in dancing school, where she was able to put me on a pedestal and show me off to the other mothers. It was when she got me behind closed doors that she would knock me right off that same pedestal; and I would emotionally fall real hard.

I realized that everything she did to show love towards me was actually geared towards getting the approval of other people. She wanted everybody else to believe she had a grandmother's love for me. Everyone believed her except the one who mattered…me. My mentally ill grandmother didn't care what I thought and she definitely didn't care how I felt.

When we got behind closed doors in her small, nasty, one-bedroom apartment she acted the complete opposite of the way she acted in public. Looks are so deceiving. I think about this a lot when I see seemingly happy families. I wonder if they are *truly* happy, or if it's an act for the public. I lived in an act, so I can't help that my mind goes there. After so many years of putting on an act with my grandmother, it's easy to believe that somebody else out there might be putting on an act, too.

Martha Ann had a deformed hand. I was told it was because her mother killed a chicken with her bare hands when she was pregnant with Martha Ann. I was told so many crazy stories about my grandmother, but this is one story that's just a little too hard to believe. Regardless of how she got her deformed hand, she liked to use that hand as a weapon to get her point across to me.

Instead of pointing at me, she used that ugly, deformed hand to get my attention. She would aim for my face to make sure that she left her marks across my flesh with her nails. If she didn't use her hand she would find anything in the house within reach to accomplish her mission to leave her mark on my body. Her favorite tool was the prong end of an orange, heavy-duty extension cord. Every time she hit me with that cord, I swear she took a piece of my skin with it. And to think I believed she loved me. Children want to believe that those who care for them genuinely love them.

I wasn't an unruly child. Well, I don't remember being unruly, and I sure don't remember being unruly enough to warrant the abuse I was given by my own grandmother. I can't imagine purposely acting out at home or in school knowing that I was going to get a beating for my actions. I tried too hard to be loved and accepted, but my grandmother made a point to remind me daily that I was going to be just like my mother. She obviously didn't think much of her daughter to feel the need to throw that in my face every day. She also failed to realize that she was speaking about someone I loved – my mother.

One day after school, when I was six years old, Martha Ann called me into the living room where she had been sitting most of the day plotting her next attack on me. I knew she was plotting because that's all she ever did. I seemed to always be the focus of her thoughts. Beating me seemed to be the highlight of her day

"Get over here and tie your shoe!" she yelled. "I don't know how to tie my shoe, Mommy," I whined. I called her Mommy because she told me to, not because I thought she earned the title. As far as she was concerned, my mother didn't exist because when I asked for her she would tell me, "Your mother don't want your dumb ass. She out in those streets doing what she want to do and she's not thinking about your bastard ass."

"Come here, dummy, so I can show you how to tie your shoe!" I walked over to my grandmother feeling frightened, knowing that I was going to get a beating. It was guaranteed. Earlier that week we had gone through the same thing with my shoe strings. When I couldn't tie my shoe, she gave me a good beating and made me stand in the corner for hours. This time she went step by step in showing me how to tie my shoe, but it was difficult for me to follow her instructions because her crippled hand made everything confusing. Once she was done, she untied the shoe and threw it at me. I wondered if she really wanted me to learn to tie my shoe.

"Tie your shoe!" she demanded. I slowly kneeled down, trembling, to try to tie my shoe. To my surprise I did it right on the first try. Again, God takes care of babies and fools. "Mommy, I tied my shoe!" I shouted. I knew that she would be happy with me, because I had been disappointing her lately.

Well, she wasn't happy at all. She just stood up and slapped me so hard I lost my balance and hit my head on the corner of the kitchen table, missing my right eye by a hair. Our apartment was small so it wasn't anything for me to get slapped in one room and end up in another room. That's how powerful her hits were. It's a wonder my little body withstood all of that force and that I'm still alive today without being crippled.

I fell to the floor and let out a loud cry while blood flooded the floor. My own grandmother set me up to fail regardless of whether I tied my shoe or not. She plotted these types of incidents in her twisted, mentally-ill mind all the time. I didn't have a chance.

"Shut your ass up! If you would've tied your shoe up right the first time, I wouldn't have had to slap you. Get your ass up and shut up before somebody hear you making all this noise." She blamed *me* for *her* abuse.

I did as I was told, but the blood was dripping onto my school shirt, which made my grandmother livid. She hated when I messed up her "good school clothes," especially with blood. When my grandfather came out from the back room to see what was going on, my grandmother told him to go back in the room and mind his business. Mr. Timid did what he was told, and he marched right back into his room. He could have helped me, but he was probably just as afraid of her as I was. The only other adult in the house couldn't come to my rescue. I was alone and afraid.

She then went into the bathroom and got an old used towel and put it over my right eye. She took off my shirt and made me stand in the corner. She was angry with me for messing up *her* school shirt, so I had to stand in the corner until it got dark. It wasn't the shirt I messed up that got her so angry. It was the fact that someone might see the blood stains and ask questions. She didn't want her private abuse to be publicly known.

We had many nights like these. I would come home from school and she would be mad about something that had absolutely nothing to do with me, and beat me until *she* got tired. Because of things she made up in her twisted mind, there were many nights that she made me go to bed hungry as another form of punishment. Those hungry nights caused my imaginary friends and me to sneak in the kitchen and eat Gomet Star's dog biscuits. I was just that hungry. I can still recall the taste of those cold, hard biscuits. They tasted like oatmeal bars with no flavor, but I got used to them and was happy just to temporarily hide my hunger pains.

Martha Ann wasn't a good cook at all. To be honest, I can't remember her ever cooking a half-decent meal. This might be because whenever she did cook she made me sit there and eat everything, whatever it was, until my plate was clear. I vividly remember her shoving a head of cauliflower in my mouth until I threw up. I wish I had memories of a loving grandmother cooking my favorite foods, but I don't.

I was so traumatized from the abuse I was getting at home that when I went to school I would hide under my desk most of the day. None of the other children wanted to be my friend or even get close to me because my body was always covered with huge blisters from untreated eczema or bruises from getting beat. Teachers didn't seem to be concerned with my condition unless I was having one of my episodes and hid underneath their desk.

The teachers just didn't seem to get it. Looking back, I don't know if they were confused, afraid of me, or just didn't know how to help me. They would spend a few minutes trying to coax me to come out and then rejoin the class. None of them felt the need to report my condition, which baffles me to this day. How in the world do you ignore obvious signs of neglect and abuse? Maybe my personal pain wasn't as obvious to others as it was real to me. Maybe they just thought I was crazy or shy. I wonder, were they that busy or did they just choose to have a blind eye and not get involved? God help the children silently crying out for help.

During summer break and school vacations, my grandmother would take me to work with her to clean up the white people's homes. In the winter months, when it was cold, she would sit me down by the hot radiator and tell me not to move until she was finished. I remember my skin burning from the heat, aggravating my infected flesh. The night before I would have been sleeping on hot plastic, so heat was the last thing I needed. She didn't care. In fact, I think she enjoyed seeing me in pain. The heat was unbearable, but I was so used to pain; it became a part of my day. I expected to feel pain in some form or fashion and the more intense the pain was, the stronger I got. I had no other choice except to endure the pain. No one was coming to help me.

I was very sickly and probably malnourished, which caused me to be in and out of the hospital way too often. Not even the hospital staff thought about reporting my condition, or maybe they thought about it and just chose not to take action. After so many frequent visits at such a young age, you would think somebody had sense enough to at least ask questions. My grandmother was so manipulative and so convincing with her lies, the hospital staff probably believed her stories.

Each time I was discharged from the hospital, I was guaranteed one of my grandmother's discipline specials for embarrassing her. No matter where we went or who we were around, she always thought of me as a big embarrassment to her. I couldn't figure out why she would want me if I embarrassed her so much. Why didn't she give me back to my mother and not be embarrassed anymore? It sounded like an easy fix to me, but who knows what was going on in her mentally-ill mind.

I remember having to walk behind my grandmother like I was her dog. When she sent me outside with my imaginary friends she would make me go without a shirt, so I wouldn't mess up my school clothes. I don't remember having any play clothes. Again, I was left unnoticed. How many young girls go outside to play topless? Surely, the neighbors were curious, but obviously not curious enough to ask questions.

On Martha Ann's "good" days, she would allow me to sit at the foot of her bed on the floor and let me watch soap operas with her. She also continued to put me in those dance classes, which I enjoyed...until I messed up the dance routine on performance nights. She expected me to be perfect, which was impossible according to her standards, so when we returned home she would beat me and send me to my corner for embarrassing her.

Uncle Gerald would come and visit me as often as he could, but it wasn't often enough for me. He would sit me on his lap and say, "MoMo, you are going to be a heartbreaker. You're gonna be a model when you grow up." I loved to see my uncle coming; he was an angel in my eyes. He made me feel pretty and he spoke words to me that made me feel special. His kind words were words I rarely heard. I was later told by family members that he was molested by my grandmother and he in turn molested my mother. I don't know how true this is because I wasn't there, but it wouldn't surprise me. After all, when my mother told me he tried to kiss her, surely it wasn't his first and last time trying something like that. I loved my uncle, but I've seen so much during my days of abuse in foster care that absolutely nothing could surprise me about what goes on behind closed doors.

One day I remember it was time for my grandmother to take me to school, and I had a bad cough. She warned me before we reached our apartment building elevator that I had better not cough while I was on that elevator with other people. I was scared to death and hoped with all my heart that I wouldn't have to cough. When the elevator door opened, I walked on trembling. I had a continuous cough that was difficult to suppress and we lived on the fifth floor, which meant I had to hold my breath until the elevator hit the first floor. I don't know why I felt like I needed to hold my breath, but I did. Right before the elevator door opened up on the ground floor, I felt like I was going to die from holding my breath for so long and hard. My chest was hurting, and it happened. I let out a big cough, and to make it worse, I didn't cover my mouth. Once everyone walked out of the elevator my grandmother grabbed her keys from her purse and ran them down my back. It felt like electricity running through my body. I was terrified that we were the only ones on the elevator. I didn't know what else she might do to me behind those closed elevator doors.

"Didn't I tell your stupid ass not to cough?" she yelled. "Embarrassing me in front of these white folks, you're just like your trifling mother. I hate your ass."

"Mommy, I didn't mean to…"

"Shut the fuck up and walk in front of me. You'd better not say one more word."

I kept on walking like my grandmother instructed me to, with my back on fire from the cuts made from her keys. My flesh was wet from the cuts and was sticking to my shirt. All I could think about was getting another beating for messing up my school clothes. I jumped in the back of the car and wept until we pulled up to my school.

I walked into school with my head down like I always did and went straight under my desk. Usually my teacher would be able to talk me from under the desk, but on this particular day, I didn't budge. I was in severe emotional and physical pain, and under the desk was my comfort – away from everybody and everything. In my child's mind, I just knew my teacher would know that something terrible had happened to me or maybe I would scare the other children enough for them to stare at me long enough to cause a distraction in the class.

Amazingly, the principal came to the classroom and convinced me to get out from under the desk and come to his office. I was relieved to be rescued. A bunch of people were in the office staring at me and asking me questions. They examined my body and found old bruises and new bruises. Once they noticed the open gashes on my back, their mouths hit the floor in disbelief of what they saw. After their long meeting and lots of questions, I was sent back to class.

Needless to say, when I got home from school that day, my grandmother was very angry. She had received a call from school stating that I was bruised up, and she promised me the worst beating of my life for "running my mouth." Usually she wouldn't waste any time giving me a beating, but this time she told me to go to my room, the dining room, and she would get to me later. I went to my room and stared out the window, wishing I could escape from this ongoing nightmare. I was weary.

Moments later, I watched this white car pull up in front of our apartment building and park. I saw a well dressed white women get out of the car and instantly I felt relieved and safe. I believed that it was God's intention to give me peace at that moment because I had no idea who these people were or why they were at our building.

Soon there was a knock on our door. My grandmother went to the door cussing because someone was bothering her. But when she looked through the peephole, her attitude changed. Now that I think about it, she was probably saying to herself, "This can't be happening again." She ran in the back and threw on her wig and headed back to the door. Before she opened it, she gave me a look of disgust.

"Mrs. Williams, we are from the child protective services. May we come in?" Politely, my grandmother replied, "Sure, sure. Come right on in. How can I help you?" I had never heard her speak so politely. I didn't even know she knew *how* to use nice words, and I had never heard the strange tone in her voice; I had only heard the tone of terror towards me. Martha Ann's entire demeanor had changed; and I barely recognized her. I listened in complete amazement.

"Thank you. The reason why we are here this evening is because we received a call from Monique's principal stating that she came to school with some scratches on her back." As the woman spoke, she stared at me with concern in her eyes.

"Now why would they call you and tell you that? I take good care of Monique. Don't I?" Martha Ann looked at me, but I kept my eyes fixed on the blonde haired lady. Inside I was crying and begging, "Please take me with you! Please!" I was hoping she could hear my thoughts, or maybe she was a mind reader.

"I take good care of her, like I said. Her mother don't want her and…"

"Mrs. Williams, it's just standard procedure that we come out to investigate what was reported. If she doesn't have any scratches on her back, you don't have anything to worry about."

She was looking my grandmother directly in her eyes now. The blond-haired lady asked me to turn my back to her and then she carefully peeled my shirt from my wounded back. We sat there in silence for what seemed like forever as she held my shirt over my head examining my back. Finally, the social worker grabbed my hand and proceeded to walk towards the door.

As I walked out the door and into the elevator, my grandmother screamed, "You're just like your sorry ass mother, calling these white folks on me. You'll be back! No one wants your stupid ass! Monique, I can't believe you did this to me. I love you so much!" I couldn't believe the words I was hearing my grandmother screaming. Love? Did she *really* love me? I wanted so badly to believe she did.

Moments later I was off with a stranger in the white four-door car. I never saw my grandmother again until I was standing over her at her funeral when I was eighteen years old.

My mother refused to attend my grandmother's funeral, but she insisted that I go. I didn't want to go, but of course I had to grant my mother's wishes. I was so emotionally detached that I don't even remember the long ride from New York to Ohio. I do remember visiting my grandmother's two-story house and it was in the same condition her apartment in New York was in - nasty. My uncle said she left New York for a better quality of life. She saved $175,000 cleaning houses and moved to Ohio in the 1980s.

I wondered if anyone was thinking about me or cared enough about making a better life for me. I felt lost. I didn't understand why I was being treated so badly, and I almost started believing that it was okay to be abused.

Years later, during my college studies, I read article after article about children who had been failed by the foster care system. I read how many children died in foster care homes, and how the stories are rarely reported to the public. Unfortunately, because statistics take time to compile, most research is usually a couple of years old once they are shared with the public.

Regardless of the time sensitive material, the fact remains that countless foster children are continually being abused, neglected and beaten in the homes they're placed in by Social Services. Because of the ongoing reports and statistics, I'm left to believe that the system is well aware of this ignored problem. The Department of Social Services and other foster care organizations make it clear that the use of corporal punishment on foster children is prohibited. Those applying to be foster parents must sign an agreement that they will honor this policy. To what degree is this policy actually enforced?

Foster parents are not allowed to use any type of corporal punishment. Some examples are spanking, hitting, slapping, or pushing. One of the reasons behind this licensing regulation is that children who have suffered abuse and trauma will not respond to this type of discipline. To them, it is more of the same and puts the foster parents in the same category as the abuser in the child's eyes. (foster parentmanual)

I didn't care where my caseworker took me, as long as I wasn't going back to my grandmother's house. Any place would be better than Martha Ann's house. At this time, I was around eight years old. As strange as it sounds, in spite of everything my grandmother did to me, I still loved her. I just felt like I needed a break from her. At the time, I didn't realize that my grandmother's alleged love for me could've killed me.

Looking back, my life was on the line every day, but at the same time I had a feeling that there was something greater for me than the hell I was going through. I had to believe that because I wanted to experience the same happiness the kids in school expressed daily. Believing there was something more for me helped me to get from one day to the next.

I guess it took a long time for my caseworker to find a home for me because I didn't arrive at my next foster family's home until the middle of the night, which was six hours after I left my grandmother's home. I later found out that my grandmother didn't have legal custody of me and that my mother had to sign a voluntary placement agreement for me to go into foster care, with the goal of being returned back to her.

Knowing this, even much later, let me know that my mother wanted me. It assured me that my mother loved me in spite of everything. Words can't explain how good this made me feel. I believe every child wants to at least *feel* wanted by their own mother. I felt stronger, and I believe if I had known this while living with my grandmother, some of her harsh abuse would have been a little easier to bear. Love can make a child feel like they can conquer the world. Unfortunately, living with my grandmother made me feel like I was lost and forgotten in the world.

I couldn't wait to meet my new foster family, The Browns. I was so anxious. Most of all, I was relieved that I wouldn't be going back to my grandmother's house. I felt like someone was giving me a present when I went to my new foster home. Mr. and Mrs. Brown were very welcoming when I first arrived. They showed me to my room, which was located in the attic, and they told me to get some rest. I slept so well that first night. I don't even think I was sleepy, but I was definitely mentally exhausted from being abused. My body needed to rest.

When I woke up, I met The Brown's biological children, my new foster brother and sister. I remember being so excited to have someone else to talk to other than my imaginary friends, although my imaginary friends were always nearby. The Brown's house was beautiful and unlike my grandmother's house, it was spotless. Everything seemed to be in place, and the house even smelled clean. Their home didn't smell like a dirty dog or cigarette smoke.

The first few weeks I was fed very well. The food tasted so good, and it filled my stomach; I was satisfied. It felt good not feeling hunger pains and not having to sneak to eat dog biscuits. Although I ate in the kitchen alone, it didn't bother me because I had my imaginary friends, who were also happy that I was in a better place. The Browns also tended to my grandmother's inflicted wounds that were all over my body. I began to feel right at home with my new family and they seemed to be happy that I was there. I didn't miss my grandmother at this point. In fact, she didn't even cross my mind. I was happy and beginning to feel like everything would *finally* be okay. I was safe, rested, happy and full.

Everything seemed to be going fine, and my case worker's visits started to get less and less frequent. Sadly, things in the Brown's house started to slowly change. The warm welcoming family that took me in their home, in the middle of the night, was no longer welcoming. The time I spent in the attic seemed to get longer and longer, and I was only allowed to come down to eat alone in the kitchen. Immediately after I ate, I had to go back to my room - in the attic. The attic was where I assumed I belonged. Because I spent so much time in the attic, I could hardly tell the days from nights.

When I wasn't up in the attic, I was downstairs in the basement. I was never told why I had to go to the basement. Maybe the Browns were trying to give me something different to look at. I don't know, but there wasn't much in the basement except some old furniture. The basement was always cold and dark with a trace of light coming from the top of the stairs, which was from a small fixture with a light bulb screwed into it and a chain hanging from it to turn the light on and off.

Every now and then, they would leave that light on. Sometimes I would just sit and look at the light. When I was cold, I would stare at the light and imagine being a moth or a butterfly, so I could fly close to it and feel the heat. Other times, I would sit for hours and imagine being a beautiful butterfly and flying towards the light that would hopefully lead me to something other than the dark basement. I wanted to fly away. I wanted to be free from the basement, but the only other place the Browns would let me go was in my room – the attic. The butterfly in me wanted to escape; I wanted to be free.

According to the Browns, there was no reason for me to come downstairs. Everything I needed was in the attic. The attic had three little rooms, with a twin-size mattress and a lamp. One of the other rooms was full of boxes, and the third room was the bathroom. The attic took on the temperature of whatever the weather was outside. In the winter months, it was cold in there, and in the summer months, it was hot. There was no ventilation in the attic, and I didn't have a fan to keep me cool or a heater to keep me warm, which meant I was never comfortable.

I don't think it was Mrs. Brown's intention for me to be comfortable or she wouldn't have put me in the attic to begin with. What else could I possible need that I didn't have in the attic? Well, how about a little social interaction and conversation with the family that took me in and agreed to care for me? I knew things were going bad. I started thinking about my abusive days with my grandmother and hoped they wouldn't be as traumatic. I was hoping that maybe the Browns would just say mean things to me and keep me in the attic. I could handle the verbal abuse, but my little body couldn't bear any more physical abuse.

I began to feel sad, scared and alone at the mere thought of having to go through more abuse. I wondered why no one noticed me and helped me. My imaginary friends were a comfort to me just by staying close by my side. I don't think I would have survived my many years of foster care without my imaginary friends.

For every meal, I always ate in the kitchen by myself. My foster siblings ate together in the comfortable den. They stopped feeding me good meals like they did when I first got there, so I stole food as much as I could. When they left me in the house alone, I had a field day in their kitchen. They had a little bit of everything and lots of snacks. Martha Ann didn't have anything like what the Browns had. I never took much, maybe a handful of cereal or some chips. If I was lucky, I would run across some candy. One day when they came home from church, they wanted to let me know that they knew I had been stealing; I guess I didn't cover my tracks well enough. I probably didn't close a bag or box all the way, or maybe while rushing to steal I left crumbs on the counter or on the floor. I don't know how they found out, but they did, and they made me pay for it. They made me come downstairs into their all-white decorated living room and chant Jesus' name and beg forgiveness. I had to do this for hours and hours. I guess it was their way for me to receive what they called the "Holy Ghost."

To my remembrance the Holy Ghost was like having an outer body experience. I knew what to do because I'd seen people do it before. My body was going through the motions of praising God by waving my hands, rocking my body, and saying Jesus' name over and over. The whole time that I was supposed to be getting the "holy ghost" my mind was scared and confused. I couldn't understand why I was doing what I was doing or why I was feeling the way I was feeling, but I didn't want to stop because I was making Mrs. Brown scream, "Hallelujah!"

Finally, she was happy with me. Ironically, after that night of receiving the "holy ghost," I didn't have the desire to steal any more food. I just remained hungry. Was it the Holy Ghost or was it fear of having to chant for hours and hours? Whatever it was, I didn't steal food from their kitchen ever again.

Mrs. Brown was a church-going woman, but she beat me a lot, for whatever reason she could come up with. Her beatings weren't as bad as my grandmother's beatings, but they were bad enough. Mrs. Brown would beat me mostly with her husband's belt and then she would send me to one of my dark places - the attic or the basement. What Mrs. Brown didn't realize is that I was already in a dark place in my mind. If she had never sent me to the attic or the basement, I was already living in a dark place within myself.

Mrs. Brown was also very wicked with her tongue. She went from hallelujah to calling me all sorts of names. And when she called me these names it seemed as though she went to the pit of her stomach to find the names. The tone she used was similar to the tone of terror Martha Ann used with me. The way Mrs. Brown balled her face up and gritted her teeth when she called me names made it obvious that she hated me. "Bastard," "Dirty Bastard" and "Stupid" were her favorite names for me. She seldom used curse words because when she wasn't wailing out on me she was proclaiming to be a Christian. I guess she thought she was doing God a favor by taking me in her home. Now that I look back at it, I believe my presence alone made her mad. Whatever she could say mean to me, she said it. She would remind me daily that my biological mother didn't care for me.

I don't think Mrs. Brown realized that she wasn't *really* taking care of me. I don't remember taking many baths, or practicing *any* personal hygiene for that matter. The only personal hygiene I remember was when she made me eat a bar of soap because her daughter told her I said a curse word. She made me apologize to her daughter while bubbles blew out my mouth from the soap. I'm not denying saying a curse word, but I just believe the punishment was a bit extreme. I can still remember that day like it was yesterday, and if I think long and hard enough, I can still taste the soap in my mouth, too.

After a few months of living with the Browns, my caseworker came to visit me. I don't know what took her so long to come check on me, but I was very happy about the visit. The case worker must have notified the Browns of her visit because their treatment towards me and their attitude changed drastically – almost overnight.

All of a sudden, I was no longer sleeping in the attic; I was in the room with my foster sister Mimi. Her room was so beautiful and pink. I was suddenly able to join the family in the den to eat *and* watch television. I knew this special treatment wouldn't last, so I took full advantage of it and enjoyed myself. Mrs. Brown combed my hair right before my social worker came in an attempt to hide the huge bald spot in my hair. She gave me one of Mimi's outfits and told me not to embarrass her in front of those "white folks" by getting them dirty.

I never understood why my caseworkers notified the families of their visits. It's almost like they knew I was being mistreated, so they gave the family time to get their act together and put on their fake, foster care friendly faces.

When my caseworker arrived, she spoke with Mr. and Mrs. Brown for a few minutes about my adjustment to their beautiful home. Once the Browns filled her head up with a pack of lies and a box full of deceit, she took me out to get some ice cream.

"So how are things with your new family? They seem to love having you there," she said as she stared at my appearance. "Okay," I said with my head down. I wanted to tell her so bad that I was so unhappy and that I wanted to go home to my mommy. "Are you sure? You seem a little sad. You can tell me anything, Monique, and I promise it will stay between us." I burst out into uncontrollable sobbing. "I hate it there, she hates me, she tells me all the time. I'm lonely in the attic all alone," I cried.

She looked at me, trying to register what I just told her and what she had just seen at Mrs. Brown's house. "What happened to your head, Monique?" "I dunno, it just itches really bad," I said between sobs.

Now her eyes were showing greater concern. She grabbed my left hand and asked, "What happened to your wrist? You have a huge gash in your wrist. Did you try to hurt yourself?" "No, I fell on a piece of glass walking from my sitter's house."

"You walked by yourself? That's about ten blocks from your home. Did your new mom take you to the hospital? It looks painful," she said, still holding my hand. "No," I said. "Well, did you tell her?"

"Yes, but she said I'm a liar. And God hates liars." *Please don't take me back there,* I was thinking while the caseworker drove me back. When we got to the house, she instructed Mrs. Brown to take me to the doctor because she was concerned about the bruise on my forehead and the cut on my wrist.

"Oh yeah, Monique is real goofy. She must have fell while playing at the school playground. Why didn't you tell me you fell?" she said, looking concerned. "I did but..." "I'll take her to the doctor in the morning," she assured my case worker. Mrs. Brown lied and the caseworker believed her. I guess I deserved getting cut; I was just trying to avoid the cracks in the concrete sidewalks. We loved playing that game.

The case worker wrote down the next time she would come by to visit, and then she left. It is beyond me why I was always left in an abusive home after the case worker was fully aware of the abuse. Now that I look back at it, she should have taken me with her because things were going to get ten times worse for me. The system has to know this happens.

Was I not valuable enough to save? Did they not have another home for me? Was it accepted procedure to leave a child in an abusive home? Is it *still* accepted procedure? God forbid.

Mrs. Brown took me to the doctor as instructed by the case worker. The doctor said I had ringworms in my scalp and forehead and prescribed a black cream to apply after washing my hair. The cream smelled like tar, but it was to be applied to my infected flesh. My hair was never washed on a routine basis, but it was still pretty, with big curls. Even with a huge hole in my head, you could tell by my long locks that my ancestors were of Indian origin.

The one-inch cut on my wrist was infected, which caused the doctor to give me a shot in the wound and stitch it up. "Mommy, please...oooowwwww, it stings...please stop!!!!" I screamed as the nurse administered the shot in my wound.

"Baby, I'm sorry it hurts. You should have told your mother about this cut when it happened. It's very infected. You won't feel it in a moment or two. The numbing medication will kick in soon," the nurse explained.

I don't know why, but I didn't bother to explain that I did tell my mother what happened. It could've been the evil looks Mrs. Brown was giving me while I was screaming for her comfort. Or maybe I was beginning to get the sense that no one would believe me anyway.

A week later, my caseworker came to visit me to see how my doctor visit went. Mrs. Brown told the caseworker that the reason I developed those ringworms was because I was nasty, and I didn't keep myself clean. She claimed she was telling me daily how to conduct my personal hygiene. Mrs. Brown's lies didn't surprise me. She always lied on me to take the focus off her neglect of me. My hair was never washed properly and my teeth rarely brushed. Mrs. Brown never taught me anything about personal hygiene. I may have bathed when I initially arrived at the Browns' home, but it wasn't long after I arrived that it stopped. It wasn't by choice that I stopped bathing; nothing was by choice.

Once the case worker's visit was over, Mrs. Brown instructed me to go and get a snack in her forbidden kitchen while she walked my caseworker to the door. I was shocked. *A snack? In the kitchen?* I sat in the kitchen enjoying my snack that I was never allowed to get unless I stole it. I sat in the kitchen for a while and wondered what was taking Mrs. Brown so long to come back in the house. I wondered what she and the case worker were talking about. When I saw Mrs. Brown walk through that door giving me the eye of pure hatred, I knew I was going to get it. *The case worker must have told my secret.*

I am mentioning Mrs. Brown a lot because Mr. Brown didn't have much to say. And if he did, I don't remember because Mrs. Brown was overbearing. Again, it was another woman dominating the household just like it was in my grandmother's house.

Mrs. Brown instructed me to go upstairs to the attic and not come down until she called for me. Hours later she called me downstairs, and I was scared out of my mind. I walked through the glass double doors, into the white living room, where I was forbidden to go.

"Look at this, stupid!" she screamed.

I stood there in a trance. I felt stupid because I had no idea what she was showing me. She had stacks of one hundred dollar bills spread out on the glass table.

"Do you think I need your stupid ass? I don't need any money. I'm doing your bastard ass a favor. No one wants you. Why do you think they took so long finding you a home?" She was holding a bunch of her one hundred dollar bills. *What is she talking about? Who is giving her money?*

It wasn't until years later that I realized what she was talking about. Mrs. Brown was receiving money to take care of me and she felt threatened that I was trying to take her income away from her. The government pays foster parents a weekly allowance for the foster children's clothing, toilettes and any other needs. They also receive a day care allowance if they have to work and a specialized disability care allowance if the child has a disability. If the child has behavior problems they will receive an additional allowance on top of what they were already receiving.

Although the Brown's house was very nice and they had nice cars, I can't remember if Mrs. Brown had a job or not, or whether she just used foster kids for her income. I think Mr. Brown was the head pastor of his church, so the income could have come from their church; I never knew where the money came from. Their son played the drums and their daughter sang in the choir. I remember going to church with them maybe once or twice, but that was it.

I was usually left at home by myself because they said I was a sinner. I guess sinners aren't allowed in church or maybe they don't need church. Maybe I was a real bad sinner, and it was just me. They were ashamed of me and I hated myself for being such a bad person. I tried to stop stealing, but I started again because I was so hungry all the time. Maybe I was a sinner because I stole food. Being hungry didn't feel good, so I chose to steal, so I could eat. I was already enduring so much pain that I didn't want to add more pain. The severe hunger pains made me weak. I felt like if I wasn't such a bad person and so stupid, I would be able to eat dinner when everyone else ate. I hated myself.

Mrs. Brown allowed her kids to mistreat me by letting them get away with mean, silly pranks, like putting salt in my cornflakes and making me eat the whole bowl. They would also lock me in the basement for hours and hours in the dark. They didn't realize that I already spent hours and hours at a time in the basement alone, so it didn't bother me so much. Even though I was used to the basement, I never let them know how lonely I felt down there.

For some reason, my imaginary friends didn't seem available as often as they used to be. I don't know where they went. They were probably just tired of all the beatings and lonely nights or tired of watching me be abused. I was beyond tired of being abused, too. Maybe I couldn't see my imaginary friends because I was always so hungry. Being hungry made me so tired.

MOTHER'S LOVE

I thought about my mother all the time. I wondered if she was thinking about me. I wondered if she wanted me. I wondered if she was coming for me. She promised me she would come for me once she got herself together. To my surprise, the caseworker arranged a few visits with my mother in the social services building. These visits were extra special for me, so whenever they came I was always so happy. I couldn't wait to see my mother and I hoped she was just as happy to see me. If I didn't get to live with her, I was happy being able to spend a little time with her.

When my mother hugged me, I hugged her back tightly, and didn't want to let go. I also held on to her scent for as long as I could. After the visits, I would try to remember her hugs and her scent to comfort me. My memories of my visits with my mother helped me to get through some of my rough days. I loved my mother; she was so beautiful to me. At the end of each visit she always promised that she was going to come and get me out of that mean lady's house. I held on to her promise.

I later found out that my mother approached Mrs. Brown on the streets and threatened to kill her if she kept mistreating me. Maybe that's why my visits with my mother came to a stop. I was happy to know my mother was willing to fight for me, but that's when the abuse from Mrs. Brown got even worse. My mother wasn't the most likable person around. It was no secret that she was a lesbian and a full-blown drug addict. So when my mother threatened to kill Mrs. Brown for hurting me, she was banned from all visitation rights. Weeks went by that I didn't see my mother, and I began to lose the little hope I had of her coming to get me. I was afraid that my mother's promise would never come true.

After a few months of misery, my social worker unexpectedly came and picked me up from school one day. I remember thinking that my dreams were coming true and that my mother really was coming back for me.

In August 1982, at the age of nine, I was returned to my mother. I was so excited to be with my mother; she was the love in my eyes! I didn't care what others said about her; she was my mother, and I loved her. I didn't care what she was doing with her life; she was my mother. I didn't care that she was on drugs; she was my mother and I wanted to be with her. I wanted her to want me to be with her. Her skin was so soft when she gave me her big hugs, and her tiny lips gave the best kisses. I felt like my mother's love saved me from a life of neglect and abuse. I was finally with someone who loved me; I was safe.

I would follow my mother around from room to room, which was the bathroom, kitchenette and living area since we lived in a studio apartment, which wasn't uncommon in New York. Although it was small it was very intimate. My mother kept our home very comfortable and clean. I was happy she didn't take after her nasty mother.

My mother gave me so much love that I didn't realize that she was neglecting me at the same time. She was a drug addict to every drug out there. I only remember smelling marijuana a lot, but she used other drugs, too. We had a lot of activity in the house - parties, parties and more parties. My mother's lesbian lover lived right across the street, so she stayed with us on a regular basis. We only had one full-size bed, which put me on the floor many nights, but I didn't care; I just loved being close to my mother.

My grandmother kept in touch with me to badger my mother behind her back and to let me know I would be better off with her than my "junky mother." Although my grandmother was poison to my ears, I loved hearing from her. She mistreated me, but I felt obligated to love her anyway. My obligation to her was because she loved me so much that she cared how my mother was mistreating me. *Right?*

I was a confused child. I didn't know the difference between being loved and being abused. To me, they were one in the same. My grandmother was in another city, miles away, but she still controlled me. I didn't know why I still loved her. I was more confused than I realized. The love I had for Martha Ann was an empty love, a love that actually meant nothing to me.

I may not have known what love was, but I had someone in my life that treated me like I wanted to be treated, and her name was Monica. Monica was my one and only friend in elementary school and she may have been my introduction to what genuine love was. She accepted me for who I was. I was happy when I was with Monica.

My memories of my elementary school days are very vague, and I'm glad because I wish I could forget all of them. The memories I have are not good ones. What I do remember is that I wasn't very bright. I can't even remember if I made it to school every day. When I was a young adult, I overheard my mother telling my uncle that I was stupid and would never make it. Now that I think about it, no one ever believed in me...except maybe Monica.

Monica lived upstairs in my apartment building, and she was everything that I wanted to be and more. She lived with both her parents and her big brother. Monica was a huge escape from my simple world. She wore the best clothes, she had the latest toys and, more importantly, she had loving parents. Her room was pink, with a beautiful pink canopy bed. I would always imagine myself with the same pink canopy bed with a lot of white baby dolls along the bed. I loved playing house and making tea, escaping with her dolls into my own world.

When I wasn't playing with her dolls I played with my imaginary friends, who started coming around again. I don't think they ever left me; they were probably hiding from the continuous abuse I was receiving. Monica's room was the room I never had. The basement, attic and especially my grandmother's dining room could not be compared with Monica's beautiful, pink bedroom.

I would stay with Monica on weekends and some weekdays when my mother had to do her extra activities. Monica let me try on her jewelry and her hair bows, and she would let me play dress-up with some of her clothes. I loved Monica's life, but when we played house together I would sometimes act out the domestic behavior of my mother and her lover; it was what I knew.

I was tall and Monica was short, so it was difficult to find an outfit that would fit me, but we made it work. Her mother was very nice. She was an example of what I thought a mother should be. She would let me eat meals with her family. Monica's mother partied too, but it was a different style of partying than my mother's partying. Monica's mother's parties were more like the party you would witness on the TV sitcom *Good Times*. My mother's partying was more like what you would see on *Pulp Fiction*. Two different types of having a good time.

Monica's mother often allowed me to spend the night with them. I would always sleep with Monica in her twin canopy bed. Feeling comfortable and safe under her beautiful canopy, I believed Monica's world was mine even though I had to go downstairs to my own life in the morning. Going upstairs to Monica's apartment was like going to another level in life - literally. It was like leaving my basement life and enjoying a better life...temporarily. Sometimes I felt like the beautiful butterfly in me had finally escaped from the attic, but I escaped to someone else's life. I still wasn't free. I often wondered if I would ever have a decent life of my own.

Monica's eighteen year old brother was around a lot and always made advances towards me, either by winking or blowing kisses. I was very uncomfortable being around him, and always stuck close to Monica. I never said anything to Monica about her brother; I just hoped he would eventually leave me alone. But one weekend night he woke me up at 2:30 a.m.

"Monique, Monique, get up," he whispered. When I woke up I saw his reflection staring at me with the street lights beaming through Monica's window.

"What's wrong? What time is it…what do you want?"I asked, wiping the sleep from my eyes. I was scared. I knew what he wanted. *What I am going to do? Everyone is sleeping.*

"My mother said go sleep in my bed," he said. "Why?" "I don't know, but you better get up before I wake her up and then you will have to go downstairs with your crack head momma."

"Where will you sleep?" "On da couch, where else?" he said sarcastically. I got up out of the bed abruptly, hoping I would wake Monica up from her deep slumber. It didn't work. Sleeping anywhere else other than with Monica was totally against my wishes. I knew sleeping in her brother's room was a bad idea, but what choice did I have?

I walked out of the dark room, through the dark kitchen, using the street lights coming through the window. I entered his bedroom and climbed into his bed. He didn't follow me to his room. In fact, he went into the living room like he said he was going to do. But I knew deep down inside that my night was not nearly over.

I laid there waiting for him to come in. About an hour later my anticipation came to an end. Monica's brother entered the room with a huge smile on his face. He pulled down his pants with a fully erect penis, without saying a word.

"Touch it!" he demanded.

I just stared at him.

"Go ahead and touch it, don't be scared! It won't bite!" he teased, as he pulled his penis back and forth in a stroking motion.

God help me! I'm so scared! I touched it and drew my hand back quickly.

"See, I told you it wouldn't bite. Now stroke it slowly for me," he demanded, as he moaned. *Please wake up, Monica!* I did what he instructed me to do. I held back my tears as I felt my private parts awakening. *Why am I feeling this way? I don't like this…or do I?*

"Hummmmmm. Monique, stroke harder and faster," he moaned. And I did.

"Put it in your mouth," he whispered into the dark room.

Oh God no!! Seconds later, I heard the light flick on in the kitchen, which was right next to Monica's brother's room. I'm not sure who it was but after they ran the faucet for a glass of water, they turned the light off and went back to bed.

"Damn, you're lucky!" he said as he ran out of his bedroom with his erect penis. I stayed awake for the rest of the night.

After that day, Monica's home was no longer my safe haven. I didn't feel comfortable hanging out with my best friend anymore. Her world stopped being my dream world, so I begged my mother to let me stay home with her. She told me that I was a big girl and that I could stay at home by myself. I didn't want to, but I did.

Every time my mother left me home by myself, I called my grandmother to let her know how scared I was being alone. When my mother found out that I was secretly talking to my grandmother, she was mortified and livid at the same time. She threatened to kill me if I reported any of her actions to my grandmother or to the police. I'm sure she felt like I betrayed her just like my other foster parents did. They wanted me to keep their secrets instead of thinking about my own safety and well-being. Again, I was confused.

By this time my grandmother had brainwashed me to believe that my mother was the worst human being on earth. The next time I called my grandmother, I listened to her closely and carried out her manipulative and destructive instructions. I wished my imaginary friends had stopped me from listening to her. I wished they had been with me when I was at home alone. Then I wouldn't have been so scared and probably wouldn't have called my grandmother. Unfortunately, my imaginary friends weren't around to help me. If they were, they weren't speaking loud enough to help me.

"Hey baby, where is your crack head mamma at?" she asked when I called. *Baby?!*

"She's gone," I replied.

"Where?"

"I dunno." I began to cry.

"Monique, I told you that your mother ain't shit! She ain't nothing but a crack head bull dagger!!!" *Bull dagger?*

"Your mother don't love you, Monique, I love you. Call the police on your mother and tell them that you want to come back home to me. I will buy you anything you want, just call the police right now."

"Okay," I said between sobs. Deep down inside I wasn't scared and I didn't want to leave my mother. But at the same time I didn't want to disappoint my grandmother.

"Okay, good. And remember, you want to come back home with me, okay?"

"Okay."

"I love you," she said before she hung up the phone.

Huh? Love? Why does she love me?

"Hello, 911!"

"Hello, my mother left me home alone and I'm scared. I want to go live with my grandmother."

The police and my mother arrived at the same time.

"I was right across the fucking street!" my mother was yelling as she came into the house.

"Ma'am, your daughter called and she was home alone scared. And it is our duty to follow up to ensure the child is safe," the white male police officer tried explaining to my mother. A female officer walked inside my mother's apartment and whispered something into the ear of the officer who was trying to calm my mother down.

"Ma'am, do you have your daughter on a probationary basis?" he asked.

"Well yes, but like I told you before, I was just outside across the street!"

"Well, ma'am, we have to remove your child from your care and place her in foster care. You can call social services in the morning to see if there is anything you can do to get your child back," he said calmly as the other officer put on my coat and escorted me to the door.

"Take her ass. I can't take care of her ass anyway. She's an ungrateful bitch. I bet her grandmother has something to do with this!! I fucking wish she would die!! Go ahead and take her! You'll be sorry, Nikki! Just wait!!"

I walked out the door with the officer, crying uncontrollably. I loved my mother but I had done what I was told to do. I was obeying my grandmother, but I betrayed the only person I really wanted to live with, my mother. I was confused more than ever. I didn't understand what was happening. I didn't understand why I called the police on my own mother. My grandmother had more control over my mind than I realized. She convinced me to set my mother up.

When we got outside, the lady with the white car was waiting on me. I got in the car, still trying to figure out what I had done and still crying uncontrollably. I noticed we weren't going to my grandmother's house. I was sure my grandmother would blame me and say I didn't follow her directions by not telling the lady I wanted to live with her.

So in January 1983, I was returned to foster care, against my wishes. I kept thinking I would have to go to my grandmother's house. I really didn't know where I would end up, but I was hoping it would be a nice place and hopefully safe. I was hoping the home would have children I could play with and maybe have a room for me to sleep in instead of a basement or an attic. I had only been with my mother for six months, and I messed it up. I could have still been with her if I hadn't listened to my grandmother. I had nobody to blame except myself.

I couldn't believe it, but I was sent back to the Browns' home. I later found out that it was reported I had "attachments to my former foster parents." *Really?* I don't know what kind of "attachments" they were talking about, but I didn't understand. The system failed me. They placed me right back into a home that they removed me from. Why?

I sat in the dark attic, alone, thinking about my mother. I was missing her touch, her hugs, her kisses and just being in her presence. I missed following her from room to room and looking at her. I even missed her smell. I felt bad about calling the police on my mother, and now I felt like I was being punished for doing it because being returned to the Browns sure seemed like a punishment! Who in their right mind would send a child right back into an unsafe and abusive environment?

As I continued to sit in that dark and lonely attic, I began remembering my mother's angry slurs that followed me to the child protected, white, four-door sedan. My mother's mean words ran through my mind over and over. I could hear the hurt in her voice with each word. I was hoping she didn't mean what she was yelling at me, but I knew she was mad at me - real mad.

Did she still want me? Would she take me back? Would she forgive me? Would she believe my grandmother made me do it? I was scared and began to cry again. I was also mad that my grandmother's plan did not work out and that I ended up right back with Mrs. Brown. I didn't know who delivered the most abuse between her and my grandmother, but I would have taken the lesser of the two evils.

I found out much later through my adoption and medical report that it stated that "the child shall not be placed with the maternal grandmother under any conditions." I believe my grandmother knew that all along while she was manipulating me to go against my mother. She didn't care where I went, as long as I wasn't with my mother. It's hard to believe that she disliked her own daughter so much that she would want to hurt her at any cost, even if it meant sacrificing my safety – my life.

To this day I have no idea why my grandmother disliked my mother so much. It has to be that generational curse that originated with my grandmother's mother, down to my grandmother and then to my mother. I don't think there was any way for them to realize that it was the mental illness that kept them fighting and hating one another. How could they know if they weren't mentally stable to begin with? I couldn't help but wonder if I was suffering from that same mental illness as a child when I called the police on the one woman I wanted to be with more than anybody else - my own mother.

Nothing had changed at the Browns' home, other than the addition of two female, teenage foster children who became my new foster sisters. For some reason they weren't mistreated by Mrs. Brown. I believe they were strong willed. They weren't weak like me to let Mrs. Brown push them around and control them. They didn't last long in her home. I believe if I had spoken up more for myself, I would not have lasted long at the Browns' home either.

As long as Mrs. Brown had the upper hand, and was free to abuse her subjects, she was happy. She was very happy with me because I acted like I didn't have a backbone. I let her do as she pleased with me. I gave her permission to control my mind and abuse my body. I cared more about keeping quiet and keeping my abusers out of trouble than I cared about getting myself out of trouble. I was a child, and I didn't know how to stand up for myself; I didn't know how to fight.

At first, Mrs. Brown acted as though she was happy to see me when the social worker dropped me off. I was familiar with her game, so her drama didn't surprise me. But once the door was shut, and we were alone, it was the same soup, just warmed up. I don't know how but the abuse seemed to get worse. That's when I knew without a doubt that I was being punished for calling the police on my mother. Why in the world did I jeopardize living with my own mother to live in an abusive home? My mother may have neglected me, but she didn't physically abuse me. She never hit me or inflicted any type of bodily harm on me. So technically, I caught a break while I was with her. *I guess.*

I expected to be put back into my attic, and I was. It's strange, but at least I was safe from the hands of abuse in the attic. I was beaten in every other room in the house, and I was beaten daily. My meals remained skimpy, so I went back to being hungry again. My case worker didn't come to visit me at all during my first few months back with the Browns. I believe she felt bad about placing me back there. Yes, I felt like my case worker was a part of my abuse as well. After all, she knew exactly what she was doing. If anyone knew, she knew. She obviously didn't care enough about my well-being to leave me with Mrs. Brown again. Nobody seemed to care. I was alone.

The question I asked myself back then still lingers in my mind today. *Why did they send me right back to the foster home where they were mentally and physically abusing me? Why?* This question haunts me. Physically, I always looked as though I was malnourished. My mother told me that she would come to the foster home and threaten to kill my foster parents because of my appearance. I was very skinny and wore clothes that always looked too big for me. My dark curly hair was always matted to my head, and I had smelly sores all through my scalp. My face was sucked in, showing my bone structure in my face, and I had dark circles around my eyes. It broke my mother's heart to see me that way. I can only imagine how helpless she felt. I knew she wished she could do more, and so did I. I wished she would rescue me somehow, but instead I continued to be neglected and abused.

Doctors, social workers and my school teachers were all mandated reporters who failed to report my condition to authorities. According to my social work research, in the 1970s and '80s, and still today, foster care numbers continue to rise. I'm not making any excuses for the system failing, but I can somewhat understand how I fell through the cracks. I was the product of the Department of Social Services' broken system.

Finally, after many years, The Department of Social Services in South Carolina is being sued for failing to follow up on cases where abuse and neglect was reported in foster care homes. It is reported that the Department of Social Services continues to operate a system where children are the victims or remain at risk of becoming victims because the system does not have enough foster homes, caseworkers are assigned too many cases to monitor all the children's welfare and safety, and the Department of Social Services is not able to ensure timely medical and mental health assessments, screenings, and needed treatment for all its children.

It's difficult to find concrete statistics on foster care abuse, but I am a living statistic, and no fact or statistic can compare to my personal foster care experiences. We wouldn't have to keep track of statistics if the system did what it was designed to do. That is why, instead of quoting facts and statistics, I chose to become a part of the solution. I wanted to actively be involved in something I not only had knowledge of, but had actually experienced.

There are quite a few organizations shedding light on foster care abuse, but I chose to get involved with Children's Rights, an organization defending abused and neglected kids. It hurts my heart to know that children are still being abused to the extent I was and a lot of times even worse. My story is nothing new. Abuse in foster care has been going on for much too long. Why? Why is it allowed? Why in God's name was I placed back into the hands of an abusive woman?

Anyway, I was back to being the Browns' slave, and their wish for my life was to make me miserable. In return, I stole food again, remained lonely and dreamed that I was in my best friend, Monica's, place again. I would have rather dealt with Monica's sex-craved brother than Mrs. Brown's abuse. It wasn't long after being back with her before my psoriasis and eczema started to flare up again. Neglect will always show its ugly face in some form or fashion, but somebody has to be bold enough to look in the ugly face of neglect, recognize it, and take action instead of doing everything to avoid it. No one seemed to notice me. I was back to the old routine of not bathing, washing my hair or brushing my teeth. I don't think I went to school during my stay with the Browns. I'm not saying I didn't go, I just don't remember the daily routine of getting up every morning and getting ready for school.

During the summer, before the sun came up, I was instructed to walk ten to twelve blocks down the street to my "babysitter's" house and return *after* the sun went down. I was only seven or eight years old. I guess those times would keep me in the dark – literally. I had no idea who the people at my babysitter's home were. I don't know if they were a part of the Browns' family or if they were working for the Department of Social Services. I simply followed instructions and walked to their house, which was dark and gloomy. It reminded me of my grandmother's house.

There was trash all over the house, dirty dishes were always stacked up in the sink, and the house had a bad odor. I couldn't imagine how Mrs. Brown would even know someone who kept their house so nasty. It was the total opposite from what I was used to at the Browns', but at the same time I was at peace being there.

In the morning, I was instructed to just walk right in the house, without knocking, and go straight upstairs to an empty room and watch cartoons. The babysitter showed her face to feed me lunch and that was it. I was left alone, but I felt like I was in heaven because I wasn't able to watch cartoons at the Browns' home. Watching cartoons helped me to escape from the reality of my abusive environment. When I wasn't watching cartoons, I was day dreaming with my imaginary friends. Yes, my friends always came with me to the babysitter's house; they would never let me go by myself. They felt sorry for me, but they were still with me. They would just comfort me, letting me know that everything was alright. We talked all the time and played games. We would act out happy family scenarios, like the ones we saw on the cartoons.

I didn't realize this back then, but I believe that my friends were God's angels taking care of me. My angels always watched over me. Sometimes they were real quiet and sometimes they weren't. It was the presence of my imaginary friends, my angels that gave me comfort.

I was always a big dreamer, especially on those long walks in the dark to my babysitter's house. I would look up in the trees and listen to the birds singing to me. I think that's how I busted my wrist on that glass that was on the ground that time, not paying attention. I always escaped from my bad situations, and dreamed of something better. I dreamed that one day my mother would come for me and we would live like the Flintstones or the Jetsons on TV.

While I was walking to my babysitter's house, I would dream that my mother would be there waiting for me, or maybe meet me at the door or on my lonely walk over there. I spent a lot of time dreaming while I was in the attic at the Browns' house, too. I can't really say I was day dreaming because half the time I didn't know if it was night or day.

I dreamed about being that beautiful butterfly and what it would feel like to fly right out the window. I dreamed of what it would be like to be that beautiful butterfly and to have people admire me, run behind me and try to catch me just to admire me. Instead, I was stuck in the attic not feeling admired at all. I felt like people were throwing me away instead of trying to catch me.

Nine months after being back in the Browns' home, Mrs. Brown complained to my case worker that I displayed some sexual behaviors toward her teenage son and that she wanted me out of her house. Sadly, I can't deny those accusations; I just can't remember. What if her son was displaying sexual behaviors toward *me*? I guess I will never know. A few weeks later, in September 1983, my caseworker introduced me to my new family, the Blacks.

When children are removed from abusive and neglectful families, they should be kept from further harm. And while foster care can be a safe haven for some, it can be heartbreaking for others. Too many kids live in dangerous situations or languish in institutions, are shuffled between multiple homes or torn from siblings. **(www.childrensrights.org)**

BLACK SCARS

Finally, I thought to myself, I get to go to a family who will really love me! My caseworker was confident that I would love this family. I fed off her confidence and hoped she was right. During the ride there, she explained that I would have a lot of brothers and sisters and that they were eager to meet me. I was anxious to meet them, too, and so were my imaginary friends. She never mentioned the Browns' mistreatment and I didn't bother to bring up the subject because I was just so excited to get out of there. I was bursting with joy and felt so relieved. Maybe somebody cared after all.

When I arrived at the Blacks' house, everyone was waiting for me in the living room. My new foster sisters welcomed me and showed me around the house, while my caseworker and my new parents talked. I think my foster father was at work because I don't remember him being there during my introduction. The Blacks' home was not as nice as the Browns' home, but the warmth and the love outweighed the difference…at least that's what I thought at the time.

After the tour of the house we all sat down in the living room to talk about the arrangements. Mrs. Black was pregnant at the time, and if I remember correctly, she was in premature labor, but she didn't skip a beat in the conversation. The Blacks were very concerned with my weight and my appearance. I told them that I wasn't allowed to go into the kitchen and get anything to eat at my previous home. Although still curly, my hair was matted to my head with huge sores underneath. I was dirty and I couldn't remember the last time I took a bath. Mrs. Black sympathized with me and assured the caseworker that she would restore my health back to good standing.

Right before the case worker left she pulled me to the side and said, "You will really love it here, and if you have any problems I'm just a phone call away." I looked at her in disbelief. At that point my trust in case workers was very weak. They never left me phone numbers to call, but they always assured me that they were always available for me. As she walked away to get into her white social services vehicle, I knew I wouldn't see her again. And I never did.

During the first few weeks, I was able to eat everything and anything I wanted. They kept boxes of oatmeal pies and moon pies in the cabinet. I drank so much Kool-Aid that I would stare into the bathroom mirror, amazed at how my tongue changed colors. I was able to go in and out of the refrigerator any time I wanted to wet my throat. My new parents made sure that I had three full-course meals every day, and snacks were readily available at my leisure. I was full, and I was happy.

Within weeks I started to gain weight and my eyes started to come to life. My bald spots that I had for the past year were finally growing hair into them. My oldest foster sister Sheila did my hair so pretty. No one had ever done my hair before; she made me feel extra special because she took time out just for me. My hair was wavy and long, down to the middle of my back. That moment with Sheila made me feel so loved. I felt so at home. I was in heaven.

Mr. and Mrs. Black owned their home, which was a typical brownstone New York two-family house with tenants downstairs and upstairs. We lived on the first floor and Mrs. Black's sister lived upstairs. Mr. Black worked at a dry cleaning company and Mrs. Black worked at a bank. There were four bedrooms, but the only bedrooms that had doors were Mr. and Mrs. Black's and a bedroom in the very back of the house. That room was for my two big sisters, Sheila and Robin. They were either in junior high or high school; I can't remember. When the case worker was there, I was given the middle room by myself because I was the next oldest. But shortly after the case worker left, that changed. Actually, a lot changed.

My sister, Rose, who was a year younger than me, was put into my previously assigned room and I shared a room with my little sister Rochelle. After my baby sister was born, she slept in the room with Mr. and Mrs. Black. We had one bathroom to share among seven people, which caused that bathroom to be nasty all the time. But I didn't care because I was sharing it with my family.

The kitchen was in the same condition, with pots, pans and dishes piled up everywhere. The kitchen floor was always sticky and the refrigerator had an unpleasant odor coming from it, but it didn't stop anyone from eating. Well, nobody except me. My food privileges really changed. Snacks and drinks began to disappear to places known only by my sisters, and they wouldn't even try to hide what they were eating from me. I asked them where they got the food from and they said from "Mommy's room." Everyone in that house knew that Pearlene Black's room was off-limits to me, the only foster child.

Gradually, the love that the Blacks had for me was declining, and I began feeling lonely again. I don't know if it was because I was displaying stupidity or I was simply not what they bargained for, but everyone's attitude towards me changed. Although the Blacks' home seemed to be one of the better foster homes that I had lived in because of their family structure, I still dreamed about being with my mother again. I longed to touch her soft skin. God, she had the softest skin. I missed my mother so much.

School was an uphill battle. I struggled in every subject. Instead of learning my lessons, I would rather dream. I was placed in special education when I was in fourth grade, and when I didn't meet their minimum requirements I was left back in the fourth grade.

At least Mrs. Black stuck up for me with this. She pleaded with the principal and teachers to give me a second chance to prove that I belonged in fifth grade with the other "normal" kids. I don't know what she did, nor do I know her agenda behind her actions, but I was given the chance to prove myself. My fourth grade teacher put me in a room by myself and gave me a timed multiplication test. If I did well, they would allow me to join my fifth grade peers.

I remember that test like it was yesterday. I believe that God was with me, because the answers were coming to me so naturally. I really wanted to pass that test so Mrs. Black might show me some love again. I passed the test with flying colors and moved across the hall to the fifth grade classroom. After the test, my family was so proud of me. I don't know if it was because I was no longer an embarrassment to them or because it was just mechanical for them to act as though they cared.

A different case worker was assigned to my case. She was the sixth one I had since I had been in the system, but I think it was typical not to have the same case worker because of the demands of foster children in my city. After passing that test at school, Mrs. Black was happy, and I was happy that she was happy. When our case worker came to visit a few days later, Mrs. Black shared her good news and made sure to explain all about how she was the one that went to school and demanded that they give me another chance.

As I listened to her, I was reminded of another time, with my real mommy, when I told her that I finally stuck up for myself and fought this girl name Keisha Spady who everyone was too scared to fight. The Spady family was known not to take any nonsense. Keisha had been bullying me every day after school for no reason at all. At that age, I picked my own battles. Keisha was a rough, ashy, dark-skinned, bald-headed girl that lived in the projects right across the street from my mom's house. When I finally fought back, my mommy told me, "She is just jealous because you are pretty. Don't you come back into this house telling me that black heifer messed with you again and you didn't do anything, or I'll have to beat your ass myself." She was rolling up a joint as she talked. I guess she had been so excited over my victory that she had to call her friends over to celebrate.

So now, in the middle of Mrs. Black boasting about what she had to do to get the school to put me in fifth grade, I interrupted her, and yelled, "I would like to tell my real mommy!" The look on Mrs. Black's face pierced my body like a double-edged sword. At that moment, I knew I would get it. We were all silent for at least ten seconds until my mother laughed out loud and said, "Sure, baby, we will make sure you see your mother. I know she will be very proud of you."

The case worker agreed to make arrangements for me to see my mother the following week. After the case worker congratulated me and commended Mrs. Black on the good job she was doing with me, she walked out the door. Well, God has always given me a gift of discernment to know what was going to happen next. And I knew it wasn't going to be good.

We watched the case worker get in her car, and then we went inside. Mrs. Black stopped in her tracks and slapped the crap out of me. She slapped me so hard that I hit the floor with my ears ringing. Mrs. Black was about 5'2" and around this time I was about 5'8". I was always taller than my peers. I would often get teased with name-calling like "Lurch" or "Big Bird," but I didn't care. Their name-calling was the least of my problems.

"Get your stupid ass up. Who in the hell do you think you are?" Mrs. Black screamed. "You trying to embarrass me in front of the white folks?"

By this time everyone had started to come into the foyer to see the action.

"You want to see your crack head mother? She don't want to see you. She gave you away, you stupid bastard!"

Several thoughts raced through my mind. *What is going on? I'm scared. Where are my friends? This can't be happening to me again. Well, why not? I deserve it. Don't I?*

"Go get my belt, Rose. I'm going to beat the shit out of this bastard for embarrassing me in front of those white folks," Mrs. Black ordered. Rose ran, grinning ear to ear.

Did I do something so bad for me to be the only child in the house to get a spanking? I'm confused. I'm lonely. Where are my friends?

Once Rose had come back with my father's thick leather belt, I had escaped into my dream. I began dreaming about the family that I would have once my mother come back for me. We would be just like the white families I saw when I went to school – happy. I didn't know my daddy, but we wouldn't need him. We would have each other. My mommy would pack me a lunch with all my favorite snacks, and give me money to pick up a bag of two-cent candies from the corner store on my way home from school.

Once I came to, my skin was on fire. I was left in the bedroom, in the dark, by myself for the rest of the night while everyone else was having a party in the front of the house. I just listened to them all having a good time, praying that someone would come back and tell me to come out and have some fun with them. Hours went by until I drifted off to sleep. When I woke up the next morning, I realized that I hadn't had anything to eat for almost twenty-four hours. I thought my punishment and humiliation was over, but it was just beginning. I stayed in that dark room for the whole weekend, and I was only allowed to eat some cornflakes and chicken with rice for dinner in the dark, by myself in the nasty kitchen.

For the next few weeks I started to be compared to a previous foster child name Shakia. According to Mrs. Black, Shakia was pretty, smart and everything that I wished I could be. She would throw Shakia's picture in my face time after time, telling me that she wished she could trade me in for her. By that time, my sisters were agreeing with everything Mrs. Black said. They missed Shakia too and wished she was their sister again.

I must be a terrible child. I'm ugly, I'm not smart and my mother doesn't want me. Maybe they will be better off without me.

One lonely night, left in the room by myself while everyone else was in the front room, I went into the kitchen cabinet and grabbed a bottle of Benadryl pills and took the whole bottle with a glass of water without thinking twice. I sat there sobbing in the room in the dark, because I wasn't allowed to turn on lights and burn electricity. I wondered why they didn't like me and how much better off they were going to be when I was gone. A few moments after I took the pills, I started feeling groggy and sleepy.

"Mommy, Monique took a bottle of pills!" Sheila yelled from the front room. She must have come back there to get something out of her room and noticed that I had the bottle of pills next to me and was about to die.

"You stupid bitch!" Mrs. Black yelled. "You want to kill yourself? Good. I'm not even going to take your stupid ass to the hospital."

I was in and out of consciousness. I was just so sleepy. *Just let me sleep, please.*

"Get your bastard ass up and walk up and down this house until I get tired," Mrs. Black demanded.

I whined, "I'm so sleepy. Can you take me to the hospital?"

"I'm not taking your ass nowhere. Now walk until I get tired. And if I catch your ass sitting down, I'm going to beat the shit out of you!"

I started to walk up and down the ranch style home, from the front door to the back room. I felt sick. I was so tired. *Why is she doing this to me?* As I walked up and down the house, my sisters mocked me.

"Awww, she wants to kill herself."

"You're so stupid!"

"You look so sleepy, you wanna lay down, Monique?"

Later on that evening, after everyone was asleep, Mrs. Black told me to get in bed.

"Thank you, Jesus," I said under my breath. And I drifted off to sleep....

WHACK!!!!!!

"Get your bastard ass up!" Mrs. Black yelled. "Since you want to kill yourself, I'm going to make you wish you were dead."

So I woke up to heat across my back from Daddy's thick leather belt. Mrs. Black reached up under the top bunk bed, pulling me by my hair from the bottom bunk bed, swinging the belt buckle loosely. When she was done, I really did wish that I was dead.

Over the next few years, things remained "normal." I continued to be an outcast from the rest of the family. At school, I don't know how but they passed me to junior high school. I was sure that my sixth grade teacher didn't have anything to do with it. She told me often that she thought I would never be anything in life, while she stared at me over her eyeglasses drinking her Dr. Pepper and grading papers.

I couldn't blame her. By the time I got into her class I was very angry. I noticed that as I got older I stayed angry. Kids started to distance themselves from me. I didn't care, though. I was used to it. I fought students and was disruptive in class whenever I felt like it, resulting in getting suspended or getting detention. I felt myself changing from hiding under a desk to wanting to throw a desk.

Once I returned home from school, I would get beaten and thrown in the back room. That was a cycle that I had become immune to. The beatings got so regular that I couldn't even cry anymore. That's when Mrs. Black would get something else even harder to beat me with. Anything that she could find, if she could put her hand around it, I was going to get beat with it. She liked to use a special wooden stick, which had the same width as the thickest part of a pool stick, with a round knot at the end of it. She called it "her knot," and she used it quite often on me.

When I was getting beaten, I always thought about my mother. I wondered what she was doing. Was she thinking about me? Did she know I was being beaten on a daily basis? Did she care? That's all I had left in me was to dream about my mother. As I got older, I had lost my imaginary friends. Not because I didn't love them anymore, I would just rather sit and dream rather than talk.

When I came home from school one day, my new foster care brother and sister were dropped off by their case worker. They were biologically related and their mother was on drugs, like mine. They were a few years younger than me. The boy, Robert, was the youngest and his sister was Kelly. I was thankful that the focus was going to be taken off me, glad that someone else would get some of the dreadful beatings that Mommy was giving out. It was like when I arrived two years earlier. In the beginning, Kelly and Robert were able to eat whatever they wanted. They were able to engage with the family in the evenings while I remained in the back room. In two days, Kelly and Robert were against me, too. I didn't care; I was used to it.

After a few weeks went by, Kelly and Robert started to get the same treatment that I was getting. Of course, their beatings never measured up to the torture I was given. I guess Mrs. Black had to go through the case worker check-in stage before she started to show her true colors. I'm not sure how she and Daddy even managed to get Kelly and Robert because there wasn't any sleeping space. I guess my two oldest sisters where technically grown because they had graduated from high school. That's how the Blacks were able to stretch the truth about the space they had available. It didn't take long for my oldest sisters to move out with their boyfriends because they couldn't follow the rules that their mother and father set for them to follow.

I was alone and in my own world most of the time, but I do know that my oldest sisters were not perfect during their high school years. But that didn't matter, because I was there to take all the heat. I think Robin, second to the oldest, got whipped once. But it didn't compare to what I was getting on a daily basis. Her whipping didn't even come close; it was a joke.

Sheila and Robin were not Mr. Black's biological children, which caused a lot of problems. Rose, Rochelle and Pamela were his kids, and they couldn't do any wrong by him. Rose and I were only a year apart, which meant whatever she did wrong I was going to pay for it. She never received any type of discipline or paid the consequences for her actions. Never. Rochelle and Pamela were the babies and that was that.

Once Sheila and Robin moved out, living arrangements started to shift around. Rose and Rochelle shared a space in the "back room." Kelly and I shared a room in the middle room and Robert took the room up front. Things remained the same, with the only difference being that I wasn't the only one to get the Mrs. Black specials. When we got home from school we had to clean the whole house among the three of us. Once we were done we ate the Blacks' special "chicken with rice" for dinner and went to bed.

The other kids didn't have to clean up. They didn't have to eat the "special" and they were able to enjoy whatever they wanted for dinner. Sometimes Mr. Black would take them to McDonald's for dinner and we ate what was in the kitchen. Rose would always get the Big Mac with large fries and strawberry shake. She would sit in front of me and slowly break a piece of her burger off and put it in her mouth, and then lick her lips.

I sat there and watched her as she ate, thinking, *I want some McDonald's so bad. If she doesn't finish all of her food maybe she will give me the rest like she did the other day.* She would eat every bite of that Big Mac, with a slight smirk on her face. *Oh well, maybe next time.*

"It's so unfair!" I mumbled under my breath as I walked away.

"What?" Mrs. Black asked. Startled, I wondered where Mrs. Black came from.

"Nothing," I said in surprise. I didn't mean for anyone else to hear me.

"Who do you think you are? You need to be grateful that I took your bastard ass into my house!" she yelled into my face.

"I like McDonald's. I just think it's not fair for your kids to get McDonald's and the rest of us don't—"

Whap! She slapped me.

"I can't afford for everyone in this house to get McDonald's. The county doesn't give me enough money to buy YOU

McDonald's. I go above and beyond what I'm supposed to do for your bastard ass. If you don't like it, you can get the fuck out my house and go live with your bull dagger mother!" I walked away, vowing never to mention McDonald's again. At least not around her.

That year we moved into a bigger house, three blocks away from the old house. It was a two-story home with an attic and a basement that was three times the size of our old home. There were four bedrooms on the second floor and two bedrooms in the attic. My siblings filled up the rooms downstairs with my parents, and I was sent upstairs in the attic bedroom. I was back in the attic. I guess it was out of sight out of mind for me. Everyone shared their large, newly furnished bedroom except for Robert.

Just like the Browns' home, there was a bathroom upstairs so I didn't need to go downstairs for anything. I didn't care about being upstairs in the attic by myself. I was so used to being in an attic and being by myself, I almost started to think that was how I was supposed to live. I did ask my mother if I could move into the bigger room, and she just told me I was lucky to have a room in her house at all. I really didn't expect to get put into the larger bedroom. I just looked forward to the rejection. It's what I expected.

My room was so small that I could lie in the middle of the floor and touch all four sides of the room. I had a twin bed, sheets, a knitted blanket, an alarm clock radio and myself. Every day I would escape, looking outside my attic window and wishing I was that butterfly that would just fly away. Nobody would know I was gone and nobody would know who I was except my mother. I would also look out the window and watch the cars go by, wondering where they were going and if my mother was in one of those cars looking for me.

Junior high school was great because I was able to get away from Rose. We never got along because with her being the spoiled brat and me their bastard child, it wasn't a good combination. My parents treated Rose like a princess, I guess because she was my foster father's first-born. I hated Rose. She was everything that I wanted to be. She was loved and got everything she wanted, and she never got a beating from either parent. She was good in school and hung out with the other kids who wore the latest fashions like she did.

At least I began to meet some friends and cared a little bit more about school. The friends I had at school weren't as popular as Rose's friends. I wasn't into being popular, so I hung around dreamers. I stopped dreaming about being with my mother once I realized she wasn't coming for me. It was hard accepting that my mother didn't want me, so instead of dreaming about her, I began dreaming about being on my own so no one could hurt me anymore.

There was no escaping Mrs. Black's fury once Rose started junior high school with me. Throughout our elementary years, she spent so much of her time running back home to tell our parents all the wrong I had done, I have no idea how she got her lessons done. Not only did she have a big mouth, but she also made it her business to show off her new clothes while I wore the same outfit twice maybe three times a week. I would just make sure I alternated my shirt and pants so my lack of clothing wouldn't seem so obvious.

Throughout junior high school, I stayed angry all the time. Every day after school, I fought someone...just because. Some fights I won, many I didn't. I didn't care, I just wanted to fight. I hated going home every day, so I would take my time walking home from school with my friend Renee Turner. Renee and I had a few things in common, which is why we got along so well. She was tall, dark-skinned and muscular, with short hair. They would call us the Twin Towers when they saw us together. Renee's mother was a single parent, which caused Renee to lack many things that other kids had. Her mother couldn't provide and my mother *wouldn't* provide.

We would meet every morning in front of the boys' and girls' club and walk to school, which was two additional miles beyond what I had already walked from my house. Sometimes those walks from school were rough, depending on the shoes we were forced to wear. We both developed sores on our feet due to our shoes being too small.

Renee and I would talk about all the negative things going on in our lives and dream about how it was going to be once we get older and got out on our own. We wanted our own apartment, which we promised to share. We vowed that we would never wear shoes that were too small for us anymore. We both had anger issues and loved to fight. The only difference between me and Renee was that she never lost a fight. As a matter of fact, everyone was scared of her. She wasn't any average teen-aged girl. She was strong and very muscular. She would help me fight battles that she knew I was going to lose. She always said, "Monique, your face is too pretty to be fighting." She was right; I was just a diamond in the rough.

"If you can reach a child's heart, you can change the world!"

Author Unknown

I'm not sure how old I was when I started seeing the therapist at the "K" building because of my behavioral issues at school. All I remember was that it was during junior high school because I would ditch my friends and walk to my appointment alone. Everyone knew that building was only for crazy people. I just didn't need the added embarrassment in my life. Mrs. Black would say, "The 'K' building means that only crazy people go there. And your sorry ass is definitely crazy, just like your lesbian mother." I wonder if she knew there were other offices in the 12-story building other than shrinks?

My therapist tried to help me redirect the anger I was showing towards kids and teachers in school. I didn't see anything wrong with what I was doing. At least I felt better when I beat other kids up and cussed out teachers. That's what they wanted…for me to feel better. Every session with my therapist seemed pointless. She would ask me a bunch of questions that didn't concern me, and in return I would ramshackle her office, just because I felt like it. After a few visits she began sitting further away from me. She would sit behind her desk and I would sit next to the door. She was a white, frail, younger woman who was obviously afraid of my actions.

"Do you like your home?" she asked in her stone-cold voice.

"No," I replied.

"Why?" she asked with a blank stare.

Why is she asking me the same questions every week?

"I hate it there because she always beats me for no reason."

I didn't feel like talking much because we went through this every Tuesday at the same time. This therapist was just like the rest of them. I wasn't happy and I hated to be alive. And there wasn't nothing she could do about that.

"Are you having trouble in school? I spoke to your foster mother and she said your grades are very poor."

"And?" I said sarcastically.

"Well, maybe if you did a little better in school, your mother would reward you rather than spank you."

Who said anything about spanking?

I got up from my seat, walked to her desk and slung everything off her desk onto the floor. Then I walked out yelling, " I'm sick of that bitch!"

During the summer of 1987, Mrs. Black made the foster children get out of the house and walk to the boys' and girls' club every morning. Rose didn't have to attend if she didn't want to, but on this particular day she showed up after she had slept in. That day was a huge event because the New Rochelle club was competing against Mount Vernon's club in numerous events.

The club's basketball couch was preparing our team for the basketball dunk contest that was taking place in thirty minutes. After we warmed up, my coach insisted that I sit out the competition because I would cause our team to lose. "You have all that height and can't even get the ball in the hoop. You're just goofy," he said.

Embarrassed but not surprised, I walked over to the bleachers and began to cry. I truly hated the word goofy.

Coach Brown was a dark-skinned, heavyset man who wore a long Jerry Curl that he wore pulled up into a pony tail. He wore a black beard and a black mustache that perfectly matched his hair. Coach Brown worked with the boys' and girls' club for a few years and was well known for his basketball expertise. Once he saw me crying he walked over to where I was and sat down next to me.

"What's wrong with you?" he asked.

"Nothing," I replied.

"Stop crying like a baby, you just have to practice."

"Okay."

"I tell you what. When everyone leaves the gym, I can teach you how to shoot the ball. Okay?"

"Okay." *Wow, he's going to help me get better. He must really care about me.*

The competition began and we cheered from the bleachers. Moments later the coach told us to move to the top of the bleachers so we could see the team better. *I can see perfectly fine.* Once we got up there, he sat me on his lap and started grinding his hips in an up-and-downward motion. *What in the hell is he doing?* Seconds later he moved his hand up under my shirt and started to massage my nipples. *I feel so dirty right now. I wonder who is watching us. I mean, I can't tell him to stop. Because if I do, he won't teach me how to play basketball. I really wish he would stop.*

I felt so alone. I knew what he was doing was wrong, I just couldn't find the nerve to tell him to stop.

"Does this feel good?" he whispered in my ear.

"Yes," I lied.

"Meet me in the kitchen in five minutes, okay?"

"Okay."

He removed his hand from up under my shirt and guided me off his lap.

"Don't forget," he said, walking down the bleachers.

"I won't," I mumbled.

When he was out of sight, I ran into the bathroom and stayed in there. I felt nasty, but special at the same time. I would peek out the bathroom door watching for him. I was afraid that he wasn't going to leave until I came out of the bathroom and submitted to him. I didn't leave that bathroom until a few hours later, when I knew for sure that he was gone for the day. *Thank you, Jesus!*

Later that evening, Mrs. Black beat me with her wooden stick because Rose ran home and told her that I was "skinning and grinning in some grown man's face."

"You're a slut, just like your sorry ass mother," she said. She hit me so hard on my knee cap that I heard a crack. It was sore for weeks, and hasn't been right since.

Although I didn't have much faith in God, I was forced to go to church every Sunday. That's where I met my best friend, Trina. Trina was my escape from reality, and she accepted me for who I was. She had just moved from Barbados with her mom. Although Trina and I had lived different lives, we had a lot in common.

We would meet up on Sunday mornings and sit in the balcony of the church together when we didn't have to sing in the choir. We would sit in the balcony eating candy and catching up on the past week. We definitely helped each other survive. Trina was adjusting to a new environment and I was trying to escape from mine.

Even though my mother didn't make much effort to come and see me, she sent me letters from time to time. In one letter she told me how she and my baby sister were doing and that she couldn't wait for us to be a family again. *I don't know how that's possible because you let these crazy ass people adopt me.* As I skimmed through the letter some more, I stopped at "your father." It's funny but after all this time I never thought about who my real father was.

"I'm sorry for not telling you earlier but your father's name is Roy Blackwell. We met in Mount Vernon, New York at Nana's house. He works for the Augusta, Georgia fire department. You have a sister the same as you and lives in the same city as you with her mother. Y'all look just alike. *What in the world is she talking about? I have a blood sister? No, this can't be true.* That night I laid in the dark thinking to myself, *who can she be? There's a girl I hang out with from time to time. She invited me to her house after school a few times. People say we look alike when we walk the halls together in between classes. But I would've known if it was her, right?*

The next morning I went to school with "my sister" on my mind. I was going to gym class with her that day, so I figured I would ask her if she was my sister. *This is so silly. What if she laughs in my face?*

I couldn't wait for our gym instructor to give us a break so I could talk to Patricia. We sat next to each other like we always did during our five-minute break. Personally, I just thought she was just my friend because she felt sorry for me. I was a bum, I didn't dress well, my grades were horrible, my family hated me and sometimes I hated myself. Patricia always dressed really nice, wore pretty earrings, kept lunch money and was beautiful.

"Hey, I have something to show you," I said to her as I handed her my mother's letter. I shared my situation with her. She finished the letter and said, "That's great, Monique. That's a start in locating your father." When she handed me back the letter, I stared at it again. "Where does your father live?" I asked. "Augusta, Georgia," she said. "So does mine. Where was he born?" I asked. "Mount Vernon, New York."

"So was mine. My mom said that my father is a firefighter for the Augusta fire department. Yours is not a firefighter, is he?" I asked, not expecting the answer. "Yes he is," Patricia said with a smile. "Oh my God, Patricia. I think we are sisters!" "Cool, I always wanted a sister," she said cheerfully. "Me too! We can call each other sisters from now on, okay?"

We both agreed and started telling people we were sisters. We hung out with each other until the end of the school year and then I lost touch with her. She went down south to complete high school and live with her father - our father. To this day, I really don't know how she felt about me being a friend one day and the next day we were calling each other sisters. But when we would meet up again, many years later, she was feeling differently about our sisterly love. I'll get to that a little later....

I started my first job as soon as I turned sixteen years old, at a McDonald's. *Yes, I can eat all the McDonald's I want now.* Mrs. Black had strongly recommended that I get out of her house and get a job. I would walk from school to the other side of town to work. Mr. Black would pick me up sometimes, depending on his mood, or I would just walk all the way home. Either way, I didn't mind. The long walks allowed me to mentally escape.

McDonald's was where I met my first male friend and when my promiscuous behavior began. He was one of the shift managers. Although he was my first male friend, he wasn't the man I lost my virginity to. I lost my virginity to my cousin who was only a few years older than me. He wanted it, so I gave it to him. He showed interest in me and I was grateful. I didn't see anything wrong with it. I mean, we were cousins legally, but not biologically.

My manager, whose name I don't remember, asked me to meet him at his cousin's house. We would have sex in his cousin's room while his cousin was gone to work at the same McDonald's. The house was unkempt, as if it was used as a cheap motel. I didn't enjoy the sex; I just loved the companionship for what it was worth. He listened to me and that is what I needed. Our relationship lasted a few months until he lost interest in me. I was saddened, but I just recklessly found my next victim.

As the years went by, Mrs. Black continued to get more foster kids and I continued to remain non-existent to the family. I would sneak out of the house with my foster sister, Rose, and we would go visit our boyfriends on the other side of town. My boyfriend at that time was in his early twenties. We started dating when I was about sixteen. He was the head coach of a local youth football team that I was a cheerleader for in the summer.

Yes, the Blacks allowed me to be a cheerleader. It cost money, but not that much. My shoes were always too small, which was one of the things we had to buy. My feet hurt so badly during the games that I couldn't properly cheer, but to be honest, I wasn't the best cheerleader. I was goofy and uncoordinated.

I couldn't catch the rhythm of the cheers or even do a full split. I always felt out of place, but I felt good being a cheerleader. Cheering took me away from the abuse I was still dealing with.

Although I was getting older, the abuse *never* stopped. I probably got fewer beatings, but the amount of verbal abuse stayed the same - constant.

All the young cheerleaders loved Coach, but he had his eyes on me. I felt special that he chose me, and it didn't take long for me to have sex with him. When I look back on those days I wasn't the best dressed or popular or anything like that. He liked me for me. He was a homely-looking guy, but he was down-to-earth and genuine. He wasn't into all that fashion and glamour, which worked in my favor. I remember how much he loved my hair, which wasn't matted to my head during this time. As I got older, I learned how to do simple hairstyles. He just thought I was beautiful, and I felt beautiful being around him.

Out of all the men I slept with, I knew this boyfriend truly loved me. He hated the way the Blacks treated me. I had to stop him plenty of times from going over to the Blacks to give them a piece of his mind. Whenever I went over to his parents' house to spend time with him, I felt that everything was going to be alright. He listened. He loved me. I felt needed. Dwayne always assured me that I would have a place to stay if I ever decided to leave the Blacks' home. I always kept those words in the back of my mind.

One day, as usual, Rose and I got home later than we should have, and Mrs. Black was waiting for us on the front porch. I don't know why, but I felt that this would be the day of my escape. This was the day I would turn into the beautiful butterfly in the attic and fly away.

"Where in the hell have y'all been?" Mrs. Black yelled. "I told Monique that I was ready to go, but she took her time calling us a cab to come home," Rose lied.

Mrs. Black looked at me with hate in her eyes and told Rose to go upstairs and get in bed. When we walked inside the house, Mrs. Black went straight to the kitchen and came out with a wet mop, drenched with ammonia, in her hand. She slammed that wet mop in my face, which caused me to fall down on my back.

"Who in the fuck do you think you are coming in my house any time of the night you want?" she yelled. "Rose is lying, Mommy. She is the one that wasn't ready to leave. She begged me to wait for her," I explained, as I was feeling my knot on my head swelling up. She hit me in the head again with the wet mop. It felt as though she was intentionally hitting me with the metal portion of the mop. "Shut your lying ass up! Rose sat right here and told me the truth. You ain't nothing but a slut, just like your crack-head lesbian mother." Whack! She made my ear ring with another blow.

All of a sudden, something came over me. For the first time, something in me wanted me to fight Mrs. Black back. I had stopped crying years ago during Mrs. Black's beatings. I was just numb to her blows. I thought about the children in school that I would fight and wondered why Mrs. Black was any different. Well, she was an adult, and my foster mother, so I owed her respect…or did I?

By this time everyone in the house started to wake up from the commotion between us. I just stared right back into Mrs. Black's eyes with the same hatred she had for me. But I think my look of hatred was greater. All of my beatings over the years from the Browns, the Blacks and my grandmother consumed me like fire and I felt like a combustion reaction was about to happen inside me. The fire must have shown in my eyes.

"Oh no, this bitch want to try me now. She's eye-balling me like she wants to do something to me," Mrs. Black said to her audience that was now downstairs enjoying the performance. Rose seemed to really be enjoying it. Mrs. Black dropped the broom on the floor and headed for the kitchen again. This time she came back with a big butcher knife, with rage in her eyes. But this time I stood up, ready to take on anything that was about to come my way. I was tired of her hurting me.

She ran up to me and slammed the knife to my neck and dared me to say a word. I stared at her with the same blank stare. "I will kill you, bitch!" she spat into my face. "You want to disrespect me after all the shit I've done for you. You are just like your mother! I should've left your stupid ass with that last foster home, you ungrateful bitch. You ain't shit and will never be shit."

"Pearlene, Pearlene, what are you doing?" Mr. Black yelled as he ran up to us, trying to pull her off of me. "She's not worth it, Pearlene, she's not worth it." Mr. Black somehow got the knife from Mrs. Black. That's when I made up my mind to leave and never turn back. I would have been dead or a fool not to leave.

I ran upstairs, packed a bag and fled out the door. I ran to the bottom of the hill, feeling my freedom with each step. I called a cab at the pay phone and called my boyfriend and asked him to wait for me outside with cab fare. It was October 30, 1990, and I was finally free. The butterfly in me finally flew away....

I lived with Dwayne for the first few months after finally escaping the Blacks' house. He moved from his mother's house into a room across the street where we shared common areas with other tenants. It wasn't much, but I had some peace of mind. Dwayne supported me and my decision to leave the Blacks and did the best he could to take care of me. He was very protective of me because he knew my pain, and he made sure that I went to school every day.

Mrs. Black sent threatening messages to us that if I didn't move back home she was going to report Dwayne to the authorities because of our age difference. Dwayne didn't let that rattle him. He just continued to do what he was doing, which was taking care of me. With Dwayne's help, I was able to concentrate on my last few months of school and make it to the end. I believe he was one of my guardian angels.

I don't know how I did it, but I graduated high school on June 16, 1991, on my eighteenth birthday. Surprisingly, my mother and her gay lover showed up at my graduation.

After graduating, I began to feel trapped living with Dwayne. I loved him and I knew he loved me more, but I just knew that there was something else out there for me other than lying around with

Dwayne. I didn't really understand what was going on, but I didn't like the feeling of being trapped. So I left him and headed for Yonkers. After all those years, I was finally going to move back in with my mother. My real love!

Truthfully, I never stopped loving my mother. I had always kept in touch with her when I could, and subconsciously I forgave her for abandoning me. Now I wasn't thinking about the past so much anymore, I was just concerned about our present relationship. I was really hoping that we could have the perfect relationship that I had always longed for. Even though I was older, I still wanted my mother.

At first, I was happy to be with the woman that I had wanted to be with for so many years. I was proud of her, too. She had finally gotten off drugs and no longer drank alcohol, which made her appear to be a happier person. That's what I thought at first. When I moved in with her, she was dating her gay lover Diamond, who treated my mother very well. Whatever my mother's wishes were, they were Diamond's command. She dressed my mother in the finest jewelry and clothing.

Diamond lived to make my mother happy, and she was my mother's little girl, Cheyenne's, godmother. Diamond made sure that Cheyenne was well taken care of. Everything appeared perfect, but it wasn't. When my mother didn't get what she wanted from Diamond, she would make the whole house miserable. One night my mother got upset with Diamond, for whatever reason, and made me sleep in the bed with Diamond. I didn't feel right sleeping with my mother's lover, but I did what she asked me to do. I always tried to be obedient. It just didn't seem right, and it didn't feel right, and later on I found out why.

In the middle of the night, while everyone was sleep, Diamond moved so close to me that I felt her breathing on the back of my neck. I was so scared. Although I was much older now, I still couldn't defend myself. I remained stiff as a board feeling hopeless and defenseless, as she hunched on my back side in slow motion. I prayed to God that she would stop. *Why did my mother make me sleep with her? Why didn't I have the courage to get up or tell her to stop?* I was so used to people doing what they wanted to do to my body, I didn't know how to help myself. I felt paralyzed.

Moments later Diamond stuck her hand in my panties and started rubbing my clitoris. Immediately, I started stretching and rushed out of the bed. I ran into the bathroom, locked the door behind me and cried silently. After an hour or so, I unlocked the bathroom door, quietly passed Diamond's bed and got into the bed with my mother. It took a while, but I did it, and I was proud of myself. I didn't let Diamond continue abusing my body. I didn't just walk away, I ran away.

The next day, when I told my mother what happened, she cussed Diamond out and kicked her out of the apartment that Diamond had furnished. It wasn't about what Diamond had done to me that upset my mother. Actually, she couldn't care less. I believe she was already tired of Diamond. She had been talking about leaving her because she was not happy anymore, and I just gave her a way to escape. She used my body to get what she wanted.

Shortly after that incident, Diamond received a large settlement from a car accident she had been in a few weeks earlier. I'm not sure how, but my mother still had access to Diamond's bank accounts, and my mother took every dime of Diamond's settlement money and went on a shopping spree. She did buy me and Cheyenne, my younger sister, some things, but her shopping spree was mostly for her own gratification.

I started school, found a job and learned to deal with me and my mother's love-hate relationship. I always loved my mother, but her actions towards me showed she felt differently about me. Sometimes she could be so loving and the next day she would be slamming doors and ignoring my presence. Any time I was home, it was like stepping on egg shells, so I tried to stay out the house. I didn't want to push the relationship. It took so long to get it to where it was, so I didn't want to shake the already weak foundation.

My best friend Trina and I would find things to get into, and many nights I would stay with her. I admit that we lived our lives on the edge - dangerously is a better word. Looking back over those days of carefree living, it was nothing but God's grace that kept us alive. We gambled with our lives and our health, but we survived. Since Trina was from Barbados, we found ourselves in a lot of Jamaican clubs having a good time. I slept with many men during this time, and half of those men, I don't even remember their names. I was still searching for love in all the wrong places. Again, God takes care of fools and babies.

One night Trina and I were out at a Jamaican house party, and my boyfriend was the DJ. I felt so special that I was the queen of the party, being that my man was the DJ and that he was twenty years older than me. It didn't matter if the house was no bigger than 800 square feet. No one even lived in it; it was just used for parties. While Trina and I were helping my boyfriend set up his equipment, I heard three loud pops. When we ran outside, there was one of my boyfriend's friends lying in a pool of blood, dead from multiple gunshot wounds.

Oh my God. It could've been one of us shot to death. What are we doing out here with this crowd? We all had to stay at the scene of the shooting for hours while the police finished their investigation. Once they were done we were able to leave. We caught a cab home, and we were thanking God for our safety, but I really didn't learn anything from that experience.

After that incident, I still continued to see my boyfriend plus another guy that I had tried to let go of before I met my Jamaican boyfriend. Boo Yoo was what they called him. It didn't bother me to see two guys at the same time because Boo Yoo had a girlfriend with five kids. They lived in the other apartment building across from my mother's apartment building. They were such a beautiful family. I would wonder what he saw in me because his girlfriend was so pretty. She was light skinned with beautiful bouncing black hair. Although she had five kids, she had the cutest shape and beautiful legs.

In the middle of the night Boo Yoo would whistle once he had gotten off the elevator to let me know that he was on my floor. I'm sure other people in the building heard his whistle besides me, but I knew the distinct sound of his whistle, and I knew it was his secret call just for me. The whistle made me feel special. Sometimes he would ask me to hold his crack that he was selling until the next day for him, and I would do so with no questions asked. Even though I was much older, it was still in me to be obedient - almost to a fault. Boo Yoo would spend an hour with me and then go off to do what he did…selling drugs and spending time with his family.

I was happy being in Boo Yoo's life. It didn't matter to me that he already had a family, and that I came second to his beautiful girlfriend. I would have loved to have had a baby with Boo Yoo, but instead I got pregnant and had no idea who the father was. It could've been my boyfriend or Boo Yoo. It didn't matter because I knew I wasn't ready for a child, so I had an abortion. I used my Medicaid card that was still active from when I was living with the Blacks. After having the abortion, my Jamaican boyfriend cut me off because he wanted to have a baby, and he felt like I took his seed away from him. I didn't care, because my heart was with Boo Yoo. That should've been Boo Yoo's baby although he already had five.

When I wasn't with Boo Yoo, I felt like I needed something to keep myself busy because he was always busy with his family. I hated being idle, so I enrolled in Westchester Community College to further my education. I'm not sure where the desire came from, but I know I wanted to do something else with my life besides what I was doing, which wasn't much to brag about. I'm not sure how, but I was able to qualify for financial aid. I didn't have any parental permission for aid, but I think I used my mother's information to qualify.

One day on the bus, on the way to college, I met a friend who also had an interest in being a social worker. She tried to keep me motivated to continue with school, but I struggled academically. I couldn't focus on my studies and where I was going to lay my head the next day. Nothing in my life had stability. Unfortunately, I was only in school for two semesters before I was academically suspended.

At that time, I came to the conclusion that college was not for me. I continued to work, because my mother made me contribute to the apartment expenses. I remember plenty of times she would take my whole check and leave me with nothing except bus fare. I didn't care, though. I just wanted to see her happy, because when she wasn't happy nobody was happy.

She would get mad at every little thing, or be mad for nothing at all. She would get up early in the morning and bang pots and pans together and slam kitchen cabinet doors. Between the bedroom and the bathroom I don't know how the doors stayed on the hinges because she always slammed them so hard. I'm surprised our neighbors didn't complain about the noise.

She could have slammed all the doors she wanted to slam because I was just happy she was in recovery from her drug habit. I always worried about my mother being on drugs, so it was a relief to me that she was finally getting help. I went to some of her recovering meetings, for entertainment purposes only. I didn't have a clue about her recovery journey other than she had been clean from drugs for almost fifteen years and had a relapse.

My mother had a one-bedroom apartment, which left me sleeping in the living room. She had a boyfriend, which led me to believe she was more bi-sexual than a lesbian. If she wasn't confused about her sexuality, I was. Her boyfriend was my age, and I hated him. He stayed at home all day sleeping and watching television. One day, he and I started to argue because he told me to clean up, and I told him that he was not my daddy. When my mother came home from work, he told her what I said, and she kicked me out. Although this wasn't the first time she kicked me out, I was stunned that she made me leave instead of him.

With no place to go, my friend Ray-Ray allowed me to stay with her until things cooled down between my mother and me. Boo Yoo visited me often, which led to another pregnancy. I think I *wanted* to get pregnant because I sure wasn't taking any type of birth control. Actually, I didn't even think about birth control; I was just having sex. I may have subconsciously wanted to get pregnant because I had a strong need to feel wanted. For the second time, I ended up in the abortion clinic.

My mother eventually allowed me to move back in with her if I agreed to watch my little sister, Cheyenne, while she and her young, bum boyfriend went out on the town. *Whatever.* I was ready to come home, but I was also tired of sleeping on the couch.

Bum boyfriend started throwing hints that I needed to leave because my mother was living in low-income housing and extra tenants weren't what she needed. I didn't pay his mean comments any attention, and continued sleeping on the couch. I don't know why he felt like he could control me, but I always just ignored him.

Boo Yoo and I were still having sex, and I found out I was pregnant - again. This time I was definite who the father was. Boo Yoo wasn't happy and told me to take care of it because he couldn't afford taking care of his girlfriend, their children and my baby. I was devastated. I was so happy to be pregnant by Boo Yoo, but he didn't feel the same.

I did as he requested and planned to have my third abortion. During my abortion procedure, they found crabs around my genitals. *I remember having an extreme itching down there but this pregnancy was on my mind heavily.* When I confronted him about the crabs, he claimed he didn't know what I was talking about. For the next few weeks, he avoided my pages and phone calls. I was crushed, and I felt alone. I wasn't in a basement but I sure felt like I was in the dark, and that nobody cared.

My recklessness still didn't stop; I continued to gamble with my life and my health. Anyone that showed me a little attention, I was ready to give them what they wanted, how they wanted it, when and where they wanted it. Many of the men had girlfriends, so we would have sex outside on the bleachers, at their home boy's house or in a sleazy motel.

I was still hanging out with Trina, who would always somehow find the men that would wine and dine her. One of her men, Paul, asked me to go out with him to have a few drinks because he needed to talk to me about Trina. A few weeks earlier Trina had told me that she caught him cheating with another woman. Trina and Paul used condoms most of the time but they slipped up a few times. After Trina was tested three times, she was relieved that she didn't have an STD.

I didn't see anything wrong with meeting Paul for a few drinks, but we had more than drinks. We had sex. All I remember is talking, drinking and the red hotel carpet. I prayed and prayed that God would spare me from a disease. This wasn't the first time that I had asked God to save me from an awful mistake. I'm not even sure why I went out with Paul. I guess I was looking for what he was giving Trina, which was time, attention and money. I cried daily, pleading with God that I would never have unprotected sex ever again.

When I found the nerve to call Trina and tell her what happened between me and Paul, she began crying and hung up on me. This hit me hard. Trina was my best friend, the only one I knew for sure that loved me. After that day, we remained friends but I could tell that our friendship wasn't the same, and never would be. Trina was slipping away from me. I lost my best friend. I didn't have Trina as a best friend, and later found out that I didn't contract an STD either. I thanked God for sparing my life from the virus. I thanked God for sparing my life *again* that I gambled with so many times. God takes care of babies and fools....

My mother continued to be my mother, miserable and mad all the time. Her actions reminded me so much of her mother, and it scared me. The only difference was that my mother didn't beat me like my grandmother did, but her actions made me wish she would just beat me and get it over with. Her young bum boyfriend was still around, and he was always in our space.

The one-bedroom apartment wasn't big enough for the three of us, plus my baby sister. My mother would leave him in bed when she went to work, and at least he would have dinner cooked for her when she came home. She loved his cooking, so that pleased her. When they finished eating they would go in the bedroom and have loud sex, totally disregarding me and my little sister being in the next room listening. Every day it was the same thing. I worked my part-time job to help around the house, but the boyfriend didn't do anything but take up space, cook and meet my mother's sexual needs.

One day my mother and I got into another heated argument about something her boyfriend told her. I can't remember what he said, but whatever it was got me kicked out of her house again.

This time I didn't go quietly. We cursed each other all the way outside until I got into my cab with all my belongings. That's when I started to feel the hatred for the woman that gave me life.

My friend Ray-Ray let me come and stay with her again, but she told me up front that I only had a week because her case worker would be visiting soon. I called Uncle Gerald who I had kept in touch with from time to time. I didn't know which way to turn, or who to turn to, but I knew I needed some guidance.

"Hey, MoMo, you alright? Why does it sound like you're crying?" he asked. "Be-Be-Because she kicked me out again," I sobbed loudly in his ear. "Oh, MoMo, I'm sorry. You know your mother loves you. She's just a little crazy like Ma," he said.

"What am I going to do? I don't have anywhere to stay, and I have to be out of my friend's house in a week." "Let me call her while you are on the phone and see what I can do...Don't say anything, Mo-Mo, just listen." "Okay," I said, trying to control my tears as Uncle Gerald made the call.

"Yeah?" my mother answered. "Diane, this is Gerald. How are you?" "Good," she said bluntly. "What's going on with you and MoMo? She said you kicked her out. Diane, she has nowhere to go. Can she please come back home so y'all can work things out? I'm all the way in Ohio, so there's not much I can do from here."

"She can't respect me or my friend, so she has to go. She left here saying that she's going to be alright, but I know that not to be true because she is too slow and stupid to survive out there in the world."

"Oh come on, Diane, that's not nice to say. Maybe in a few days y'all can talk. Please?" "Gerald, I don't want to hear anything else about that girl. I gotta go." She hung up. *She thinks I'm stupid? Everyone thinks I'm stupid.*

"MoMo, give it a few days and we will call her back. Your mother has lost her mind. She is so much like Ma, it isn't funny." After I thanked Uncle Gerald and said goodbye, I hung up the phone and fell to my knees, sobbing.

God, if you're listening, I have no idea what to do. I don't have anywhere to go. Please God, help me...Please God, help me...I'm so alone right now, I need you. Please, please, please God, don't leave me. Amen.

When I was finished with my prayer, I was able to lie down on the couch and fall into a deep sleep. I wasn't a religious person, but I knew God was always there for me, and He was there for me again this time.

When children cannot return home to their families, child welfare systems must move quickly to find them alternative homes. As time goes by, the prospects for landing in safe, loving, permanent homes grow dimmer for foster youth. Many will simply "age out" of the system when they turn 18, without a family and without the skills to make it on their own. (www.childrensrights.org)

DEAR DADDY

I was secretly wanting to have a relationship with my unknown father, and my mother had thrown me out for the last time. I had enough of being kicked out, and not feeling wanted, so with no place to go I called the Mount Vernon Army recruiting station and made an appointment with one of the recruiters. I have no clue where I got the idea of going into the military. Looking back, I realized that it was my destiny to join.

I didn't do well on the ASVAB test, which is a requirement to get in the military, so the only jobs that were available to me with my scores were working in the military kitchen or being a truck driver. After my recruiter made a few phone calls, and after some begging by me, my new job in the Army was Administrative Specialist. A few weeks later, after sleeping with my recruiter, I was shipped off to basic training. May 20, 1994 was the beginning of my new life. I was reborn at the age of twenty.

Basic training was really rough for me. All the constant yelling put me in a state of depression. I took everything the drill sergeants did and said personally. I was scared and I didn't have anyone to reach out to when they gave us the opportunity to make phone calls. I called my mother once or twice during the weeks of training, but that sure didn't help much. She really didn't have anything positive to say or encourage me to keep going. I wanted to quit. I found every task difficult, but those same tasks were a breeze for my battle buddies. The drill sergeants would ask if I was "slow" when I couldn't catch on to a simple task. *They know?* I was always the one who had to stay behind when everyone else got to enjoy his or her free time. I got tired of the degrading treatment.

I don't know how, but somehow I made it through basic training, and my mother actually came to my graduation. She even said she was proud of me. *I guess.* I could never tell what her real motives were behind her actions.

Making it through basic training was just the beginning of my uphill battle in the military. Although I was finished with all the yelling and humiliation, I still had to follow someone else's rules. *Again.* When my supervisors told me what to do, I took it personally. I was angry and defiant for no reason. I just hated authority. I hated being made out to be the one who did it all wrong. Stupid. Always the one making the mistakes in the squad.

My first duty assignment was in Germany, and being in a foreign country did not help my anxiety. I was making good money, much more than I had ever made from any of my part-time jobs before the military. Unfortunately, I spent most of my paychecks, if not all of it, on alcohol, partying and my new boyfriend William. I ran up my shiny, new credit cards buying William anything he wanted. I wanted him to love me, and I believed if I just continued to buy his love he would stay with me, and not stray away. I guess I was just desperate. My desire to be loved and wanted by someone never left. Actually, my desire seemed to grow stronger as I grew older.

William promised to marry me once we got back to the States, and he even bought me a cheap engagement ring to prove his love. It didn't matter how much the ring cost. I had a ring, which meant somebody wanted me. I felt loved. Although William was "separated" from his wife, he said we had to be "discreet" about our relationship. He talked to his wife often, but claimed they were only discussing his little girl. I didn't care; I knew he wanted to be with me because we spent all our time together.

After two years of being together in Germany, William's tour was up and he was transferred to Fort Campbell, Kentucky. He insisted that I follow him there when my tour in Germany was up, so we could get married. I had twelve months left in Germany, but I didn't waste any time calling my assignment manager and pleading for him to send me to Kentucky when it was time. I knew that year was going to be a long year of waiting, but William was worth the wait. After William left, I had a few weeks leave and decided to go home. There was someone else still on my mind....

At first my mother seemed happy to see me, but it wasn't long until she returned right back to the Diane James that I was truly starting to despise. But like I said, I had someone else on my mind those days, but it was not my mother.

One evening I walked into my mother's room and, like always, she was lying in there in the dark in total silence. Any other day, I would've walked out and left her alone in her own misery, but I longed for the answer to the question I was about to ask her.

"Ma, who is my father?"

"I told you already, his name is Roy Blackwell. His family lives in Mount Vernon in the projects. Look in the phone book under Freddie Blackwell, that's his father's name." She turned over, away from me.

Below is a letter I wrote to my father, yet I never mailed it.

Dear Daddy,

The little girl in me needs to speak with you. Do you have a moment? She promises she won't take too much of your time. My name is Monique, and I'm your daughter. My mother had to leave me with my grandma because she doesn't want me anymore. My grandma keeps beating me and leaving bruises on me. Do you think your mommy will let me stay with her? I don't get fed often, so I sneak up under the kitchen cabinet and eat Gomet Star's dog treats. He don't mind though. He's a nice puppy.

Where are you? I think I need some of that clear stuff Grandma makes me drink until I get really sick. She says it's good for me, but I don't know why I throw up. I'm so stupid! My skin burns really bad. Grandma told me not to scratch, but I can't stop. Daddy, please make it stop before she beats me again.

Uh-oh, I need to go to the hospital. My grandmother just busted my face open because I forgot how to tie my shoes. How can I be so stupid? She showed me once before. When you do come for me, please don't be mad at her. She really didn't mean it, it's my fault...

Maybe you can come today because I was in the principal's office getting my grandmother in trouble. She told me not to cough and embarrass her in the elevator, and I did. How can I be so stupid? Again? Well, I guess you'll come and find me tomorrow because I see the white car outside the window...

I'm with a new family now. It's not too far from Grandma's house, so you won't have trouble finding me. I hope it won't be long because I'm very cold and lonely in this attic. I'm locked in the basement today for stealing snacks from their big beautiful kitchen. I promise I didn't mean to make Mommy mad at me.

I can tell she hates me now. She scares me when she looks at me. She hates when I look at her. When you come for me, you will see the marks from my beating last night. Mommy likes to use that orange long heavy string, just like Grandma did. I deserve it, so please don't get mad. I wish I wasn't so stupid because these spankings really hurt me. I don't deserve to eat with the other kids. So I eat in the kitchen alone for my daily meal.

Now my scalp is itching really bad and my hair is starting to fall out. I was wondering when you come for me, can you take me to the doctor? Oooo, my forehead is itching now. That's okay, my mommy took me to the doctor and they told her I have ring worms. She even washes my hair now. I think she loves me now, so you can finish what you're doing and then come for me....

Oops, I made Mommy mad again. I'm not sure what I've done but I'm back in the basement again. Even my brother and sister is mad at me because they made me eat salt with my cereal this morning. I feel lonely. I feel like a dummy. I guess this is how it feels to be dumb. My grandma and Mommy tell me all the time that I'm a dummy. Well, my mommy is kicking me out today. She caught my older brother on top of me playing house. I see the white car again. I wonder if your car is white.   Well, I'm moving again. I'm looking for your car while my friend in the white car takes me to my new mommy's house. Do you see me? I hope so. I need you to find me.

I met my new family today. I guess it's okay if they call me their daughter until you come and get me. They say I can eat whatever I want. My new mommy also said that she's gonna make my hair pretty again. I have a lot of sisters and brothers. Some of their mommies don't want them either just like mine doesn't. I feel bad for them because their daddy doesn't want them either. Can they come home with us? Where do you live? Will I have my own room? I hope so because my new mommy has my bedroom in the attic away from the other kids.

My mommy tells me that my real mommy doesn't want me because she likes other girls and she's a crack head. She tells me all the time I'm gonna be just like my mommy. I don't like when she tells me that. I don't want to like girls or be a crack head. My mommy said she was coming for me when I lived at my grandma's house. Are y'all together? I guess my grandma is right, my real mommy hates me. She told me again when she called me today to see how I was doing. She may have treated me like she hated me, but I deserve it...

Hi Roy, today's my 18th birthday. Over the past few years a lot of things have happened. These awful people adopted me. I realized over the years that you are as sorry as my mother. Just in case you wanted to know, they mistreated me. They beat me. They called me stupid, dumb, mentally retarded, mother fucker, doofus, bastard and whatever else came to their minds. They talked about my mother's drug addiction and sexual orientation daily, swearing I would be just like her. Fuck her! Do you know she ended up having another baby? She had a daughter while I was living in hell. Everyone in New Rochelle knew I was being mistreated. I mean they had to know, I walked around with bruises and too small clothes all the time. I was never happy and tried to fight anyone who came my way. I hated everyone just because. I ran away a few times. I tried killing myself once. I lost my virginity to my cousin at the age of sixteen. After him, I slept with a few other guys.

Oh yeah, I met your daughter in middle school. It was nice to hear that you were alive and doing well. You were doing so well, you were able to send for your daughter after middle school. Humph! I'm glad you gave her the opportunity to do well in school because I didn't learn shit. I feel dumb as hell!! As of right now, I don't know where I'll end up. If I can predict the future, the following will happen: I will continue to sleep with multiple men that don't love me. I'll escape getting the HIV virus more than once. I will become an alcoholic to take away the pain. I will manipulate all my relationships because I won't trust anyone. I will eventually get my life together, but I will remain mentally messed up because I have to start from the beginning learning about LIFE - things that my mother and father neglected to do.

Well, I don't have much more to say to you. To be honest with you, I hate you and I don't even know who you are. Not my fault. It is what it is.

Your bastard ass child.

"I'm glad you're looking for your father. Hell, I don't know mine. I guess it would be nice for one of us to know who their daddy is," she said. "And while you're there, ask his ass for some child support money."

What? Child support money?

I looked through the phone book, eagerly searching for Freddie Blackwell. There it was, with an address and telephone number. It took me a few moments to gather myself to make the call. *What if they hang up on me? What if it's the wrong number? What if my mother gave me the wrong name just to be spiteful?*

"Hello," a man answered.

"Hello, is Roy there?" I asked. *Stupid, he is in Georgia!*

"Roy don't live here, he lives in Georgia. Who is this?"

"This is Nikki. I think I'm Roy's daughter."

"This is who? Who is your mother?"

"My mother is Diane. They met in Mount Vernon years ago. Listen, I don't want anything, I just want to meet my father. I'm a grown woman in the military, so I'm not asking for any money."

"Hold on, hold on, let me get your number and I will call you right back." I could hear him scrambling for a pen and a piece of paper, and I gave him my number.

"Okay, I'm going to call you right back. And…uh…I am your Uncle Alfred. I hope to meet you soon."

Okay, that went well, right? But what if he doesn't call me back? Why couldn't this uncle just give me my father's number?

A few moments later, the phone rang.

"This is Roy Blackwell. Is this Nikki?" the man asked.

"Yes it is," I said. My heart just stopped. *Is this really my daddy?*

"How are you doing?" he asked.

"Fine."

"My brother just called me and told me that you said I'm your father. What's your mother's name?"

"Diane James."

"Hum, I remember Diane. It was so long ago. How old are you?"

"Twenty-one."

"Wow, you're a young lady."

"Yep."

"So I hear you're in the military? Where are you stationed?"

"Germany. I've been over there for over a year now. I just came home for a couple of weeks. I'm due to return to Germany this weekend."

There was an awkward silence for a few seconds.

"Well, I would like to keep in touch with you. You can always write me to let me know how you're doing. And I will write you back."

"Okay, sounds good."

"Let me give you my address."

I wrote down his address with such excitement that I didn't realize that he had given me his P.O. Box.

"It was nice speaking with you," he said.

"Same here."

What I had been waiting so long for was over within five minutes. *I can't wait to get back to Germany. I have so many questions to ask him.*

I went into my mother's room to tell her that I talked to my father. *Wait, we didn't establish that I am his daughter, did we?* She said she was happy for me but deep down inside, I knew she felt some resentment or even jealousy.

I took a hot shower and got ready for bed. I was coming down with a terrible cold and my head was spinning. Right before I closed my eyes, my phone rang.

"Nikki?" It was him calling back.

"Yes."

"Are you busy tomorrow evening? My family would like to meet you."

Did I hear him right?

"Ah, no, I don't have any plans."

"Do you know how to get to Mount Vernon?"

"Yes, the number 7 bus stops right in front of my mother's apartment building and goes straight to Mount Vernon."

"Okay, take this address down. They will be waiting for you at my mother's house tomorrow at 6 p.m."

I wrote the address down and said goodbye to Roy. Then I turned the lights off and lay down. *I am about to meet my family!*

I woke up the next morning feeling like someone had beaten me over the head with a baseball bat. My nose was stuffy and my throat was beginning to become scratchy. I turned on the TV and began watching from the day bed I slept on in the living room.

Today is the day that I finally meet my family. Wait, we still haven't confirmed that Roy is my father. I'm not going to get my hopes high to be let down. Hell, I may not go anyway. My head is killing me.

A few hours later my mother stumbled out of her room.

"So what's going on?" she asked. I could tell that she couldn't care less.

"I'm supposed to meet his family in Mount Vernon this evening, but I don't feel well."

"You talked to him?" *Oops, I forgot to tell her.*

"Yep, he called me last night, we talked for a few moments, then he gave me his address and that was it. Until he called me back moments later, asking me to meet his family."

"Oh, really! I hope you're not going to meet that bitch of a mother of his. She called me all kinds of names when she found out I was pregnant with you. She made it clear that her son was going to marry his expecting girlfriend."

"Humph," I sighed.

"I got pregnant with you at my foster mother's house. Somehow or other, Nana is related to your father and he was over to the house for a big family gathering. We snuck off and went under the house and had sex. Your father was four years older than me. I was 16 years old and he was 20. Technically, he raped me." She was pacing the living room floor as she spoke.

"Raped?"

"Well, that was my first time having sex. He should've known better."

So he didn't rape you.

"After she called me all those names and threatened me that if I came near her son she would kill me, I never mentioned it again. I spoke with your father's uncle, uncle Thomas, from time to time. He was the only that believed me."

"Wow."

"Anyway, he ended up marrying his pregnant girlfriend and they carried on like a perfect family." She seemed very sad as she recalled those memories.

"Yeah, I met Patricia in junior high school, but I haven't seen her since. People said that we looked alike, but I don't know for sure if that's my sister."

"I hear that. Well, enjoy meeting your new family. I'm going to bed."

She slammed the door behind her. I was used to her slamming doors, pots or anything else that she could get her hands on, so I just braced myself for the loud impact like I always did....

I was nervous as I approached Roy's grandmother's building, so nervous that I almost passed out. My head was killing me from my head cold and I had developed a bad cough within the past few hours.

Why I am I here? I feel like crap.

When I walked up to the elevator, I didn't see anyone waiting for it. Within seconds, there were five other people waiting for the same elevator. *Please hurry up, elevator. I don't want to cough on these people. Last time I coughed on someone in an elevator, my grandmother left permanent marks on my back.*

"Nikki?!?" A lady called my name, trying to get past the patrons waiting for the elevator. "Yeah," I said. *Who is this woman?*

"I knew that was you. Are you heading upstairs to Pearl's apartment on the fifth floor? *Pearl, I guess that's her name.*

"Yes, I am."

"Oh my God, you look just like Patricia. I knew that was you when you stepped out of the cab. I'm your Auntie Sarah."

"Oh, okay, nice to meet you."

"Oh my God, you sound just like Patricia." We stepped into the elevator.

"Everyone is waiting for you upstairs, but of course I am running late," she explained.

Oh my God, how many people are upstairs? It was too late for me to turn around now.

We both got off the elevator and headed towards Roy's mother's apartment.

"You ready?" she asked.

"Yep."

When we walked in, everyone stopped dead in their tracks and just stared at me.

"Here she is! I found her on the elevator. Don't she look just like Patricia?" Auntie Sarah announced.

In that moment, my body was there, but my soul was detached. I kept playing the words she had said over and over in my head.

"I knew she was out there, but I just left it alone. She is definitely Roy's daughter. She looks just like him. I figured she would pop up sooner or later."

What the fuck did she just say? She knew? So my mother was telling the truth.

After hugging my aunts, uncles and cousins for the first time, my grandmother called my father.

"Roy, she looks just like you. You can't deny this child," she said over the phone. *You have some nerve. YOU denied me and had the nerve to say it to my face.*

"Yes, Roy, she is definitely part of this family. She looks and sounds just like Patricia," my aunt said after my grandmother passed her the phone. Then she said to me, "If I would've known that you were out there, I would've took you in myself. I always wanted me a little girl."

"Well, I met Patricia in junior high school. Didn't she tell you?" I asked.

"No!" everyone chimed in.

"You mean to tell me that Patricia knew who you are and she never told her father? I can't believe this. Let's call Patricia right now," my aunt insisted, and she immediately dialed the number.

"Hey Patricia, guess who's here?" Auntie Sarah said.

"Nope, nope and no," she responded as Patricia apparently made some guesses. "Your sister Nikki is here!"

"Nikki!!"

My name was Monique when I met her. When I left the Blacks' home and moved in with my mother, my mother insisted that I use the nickname she gave me years ago. To this day, I hate that name Nikki.

"Tell her Monique. My nickname is Nikki. It was given to me by my mother," I interjected.

"She said you knew her by Monique," my aunt reported.

There was a long pause.

"Hello!! Patricia, are you there?....You knew Monique? Child, why haven't you told your father about her?"

There was another long pause.

"Well, why didn't you believe her?" Sarah said.

"Listen, don't be jumping on Patricia's case," my grandmother interrupted. "How was she supposed to know that she was Roy's daughter? Hell, when I heard about it, I didn't believe it either. That's why I told Roy to ignore all the rumors, because Janet and Roy belonged together."

No she didn't! I can't believe she said that shit again.

I was burning up inside. My grandmother had just made it clear that Patricia was her baby, and my coming into the picture was going to be a problem. During my entire visit, she just sat there behind the scenes, staring at me. Deep down I knew this was one problem that would not be going away.

After we took tons of pictures, and after me listening to them talking about what would've and what could've, I was ready to go home. The later it got, the sicker I felt. I said my goodbyes, promised to keep in touch and took a cab home. But my visits with this new family were not over. The next day, my father called me again. This time he offered to pay for my flight to Georgia, so he could finally meet his daughter.

On the plane ride to Augusta, I had two Bacardi and Cokes to ease my mind. I was ready to ask a lot of questions, and I wanted straight answers. Since his mother claimed she knew about me, then he must have known about me too. *From now on she will always be my father's mother to me.* I started to get angry but decided to let it go and enjoy what awaited me at the gate. It seemed as though I was the only one in the airport waiting for a ride. The drinks I had two hours earlier began to wear off.

Moments later my father walked through the door with a huge smile and gave me a big hug.

"Welcome, daughter…I can't deny you if I tried. Whew, you look just like me and your sister. Oh my goodness," he said, and he kept repeating this on the ride home.

"I seen your mother in Mount Vernon on 4th Ave when your were a baby in the stroller. I told her that I heard the rumors about you being my child. She said that I wasn't the father and that her boyfriend was the father. So I left it alone. I even took a peep in the stroller."

Didn't I look like Patricia? You didn't see any resemblance to the family or you? Or did you believe what you wanted to believe, what your mother told you?

I don't remember much about the ride to my father's home. I just remember being overwhelmed with the resemblance between us. On the way he took me to different homes to introduce me. I even remember one woman asking me if he was sure I was his. *What does it look like?* Everyone else was very welcoming and amazed at our resemblance.

Once we finally made it home, I met my little brother and sister. They were so excited to see me.

"Oh no, not another sister!" my brother said, running out of the room jokingly. Alexander was 10 years old, and my sister Olivia was 6. My stepmother, Carol, invited me into her home with welcoming arms.

"Roy, you need to be ashamed of yourself. She looks just like you," she giggled after giving me a hug and the up and down look over.

Patricia was home from college visiting our father. Ironically, we had on the same color shirts and a similar hairstyle, which made us look like identical twins. Patricia hadn't changed much since the last time I had seen her in junior high school. She still dressed nice, though her hair was longer.

Patricia was not as thrilled as the others to see me. As of matter of a fact, I think she said two words to me, "Hi" and "Bye."

After my father took what seemed like a million pictures of me with himself and my siblings, we sat down and ate the dinner Carol prepared for us. Early the next morning, he took all of his children on what seemed like another round-robin, showing off his new-found beautiful daughter. If he had only known that I was a diamond in the rough. Our last stop was at my Aunt Janice's house. Her husband, my father's uncle, had passed away just a few years earlier. She was happy to see me but mad at my father for her being the last stop.

"Roy, she looks just like you," she said.

"I know, I can't deny her if I tried," he chuckled.

"You know, Roy, before your uncle passed he told me that Nikki was out there somewhere and if she ever showed up to accept her with open arms."

Not another one knowing about me and just sweeping me under the rug.

"Say what?" my father said, with a confused look.

"Roy, I would've told you but he made me promise not to say a word about it," she explained.

"Humph."

"He told me that Nikki's mother told him that she was pregnant with your baby. But he said Pearl was trying not to hear that. He tried to talk some sense into her, but she wasn't budging. She was adamant that you marry Janet."

My hatred for that woman, my father's mother, instantly grew even stronger than it was when I was sitting in her living room.

"Well, she is here now, and we can't change the past. We can only move forward," he said as he continued to take pictures of his love child.

And that's what everyone did. Moved forward. But as for me, I still needed some questions answered. I just didn't know if anyone would ever listen to them.

I felt confused in my heart and in my mind. So much happened in such a short time that I didn't know what or who to believe. I wasn't even sure whether to believe my mother or not. She spent most of her time getting high, so maybe she didn't remember who my father was. What if she was wrong? They said I looked like my father, and although he was happy to see me, I still had doubts. There was a chance that my mother was wrong when she pointed me in the direction of the man that was supposed to be my father.

AFTERMATH

As it turns out, years after my foster care experiences and when I was married with my son, my mother came to visit me. While we were talking and revisiting the past, the subject of my father came up. When I first inquired about who my father was, I remember her clearly telling me that my father was the only man she had ever slept with. Well, she changed her story and told me that she slept with someone else before my father. We laughed about it but deep down inside I felt betrayed...again. All these years I pointed the finger at my father's family for leaving me stranded but my mother's promiscuity led them to believe that I wasn't his. She wasn't a slut like my grandmother claimed her to be but she had her right to have her reservations about my mother.

When I returned to Germany after meeting Roy and his family, the emails and phone calls from William became less and less frequent as the weeks went by. I called him four to five times a day. He never seemed to be available, but that didn't stop me from blowing up his phone. When I did get in touch with him, he would convince me that I was overreacting and promised that when I got to Kentucky, things would be better. I was still depressed by the lack of attention I was getting from him, but I held onto the hope that we would one day be married.

Thankfully, in exactly twelve months, my assignment in Kentucky came through. I was so happy! William and I would finally be together and would soon get married. The day came, and I arrived in Kentucky. William and I were reunited, and things seemed to go back to normal for us, just the way they used to be. I continued to spoil him with lavish gifts, and he continued to take them. I didn't care that I wasn't getting gifts in return. My gift was being with William; that was enough for me. I just wanted him to be with me, so if that meant going into debt for the man I loved, so be it.

After a period of impulse spending and splurging, my money started to run out. I didn't have the money that I used to have, and that seemed to irritate William. He started going out without me, promising that he would come back to my barracks room when he got through with his partying. Sometimes he kept his promise, and sometimes he didn't. I continued to hold onto my hope of us getting married. I knew he would one day be coming home to me every night.

After awhile, I began feeling really tired, and my stomach started cramping really bad. *I know I'm not pregnant, I haven't missed a pill. Have I?* After a week, I couldn't bear it anymore, especially after noticing a smelly discharge. The sergeant had us running five to six miles daily and the pain in my stomach was taking a toll on me. I was in shape, but the pain had me feeling like I was in the worst shape of my life. I felt miserable. The pain got so bad that I made an appointment to see the nurse practitioner. I got a full woman's examination, and the nurse examined me thoroughly. *I know it's just a urinary tract infection.* Twenty minutes later, she came back into the room.

"Baby, you have Chlamydia," she said in a point blank voice. She was a short African American woman in her early 50s. By her demeanor, I knew that she didn't take much crap from anyone.

"Chlamydia!!! What is that?" I asked. "It's a sexually transmitted disease," she said patiently. "Well, how did I get that? I only sleep with one guy."

"Well, baby, you got it from him." "No, he didn't give me this. We are always together. We are going to get married. He loves me." "Baby, let me tell you something. A man will be a man. You can't stop them from doing what they are going to do. You are a beautiful girl. I see women like you every day, in denial about their mate giving them an STD. My advice to you is to tell your boyfriend your diagnosis and encourage him to go see the doctor so he can begin taking some antibiotics."

She wrote out my prescription. *I can't believe this is happening to me. I must have gotten this by sitting on those nasty toilets in the barracks. There is no way William has given this to me. He loves me. This lady doesn't know what the hell she is talking about!*

As the nurse was walking out the door, she said, "Take care of yourself" and she shut the door behind her.

I boldly confronted William as soon as I left the doctor's office. He was just as bold, and convinced me that he hadn't been cheating on me. *I knew that nurse didn't know what she was talking about. William loves me.*

As the months went by, I saw less and less of William. I knew our relationship wasn't as strong as it used to be, but I held on to what was left of it. He got promoted to sergeant and was able to move off post to an apartment. One night William promised me, like he always did, that he was going to come spend the night with me after he was finished partying. He and I used to go partying together, but he said he needed some space to hang out with his boys. I believed him, and reluctantly gave him his space.

I waited and waited for William to come by my barracks room. The hours slowly went by while I waited for a knock on my door. After 3 a.m. rolled around, I accepted that William was not going to keep his promise; he wasn't coming to see me. Without even thinking about it, I quickly grabbed my keys and jumped in my car, in my pajamas. I was headed right to William's apartment. I was on a mission and nothing was going to stop me from finding him. I needed answers. I spotted his truck parked in his parking spot in front of his apartment complex, so I knew he was home because wherever he was, so was his truck. He loved that truck, and all the upgrades that I had done to it to make it stand out.

He must be asleep or drunk from hanging out with the boys and didn't want to risk the chance of coming through Fort

Campbell's military police intoxicated. Maybe he didn't want to wake me because it was so late.

I parked my white, five-speed Beretta and ran upstairs to his apartment. I didn't know what to expect, but I knew I would see William. When I got to his door, I heard some laughter and music playing inside. My heart sunk. *Is that a girl's voice?*

I knocked on the door, and William answered within seconds. It was like he was expecting me to come.

"What are you doing here, Nik?" he asked.

"What's going on, William? Who is she?"

As I began to cry, that woman just sat on the couch looking at me with so much confidence, and a smirk on her face. *She is beautiful.*

"Nik, I told you that I needed some space. As a matter of fact, I don't want to be with you anymore. You don't trust me and I am tired of being accused of cheating and arguing all the time. I'm moving on and I expect you to do the same." He sounded so harsh. He didn't sound like the William I knew, and he definitely didn't sound like the William I was going to marry.

"William, please don't do this to me. I love you and I will buy you anything you want. Just please don't do this to me."

"Nik, you don't have any more money. Please leave before I call the cops."

"Oh no, William, please don't do this to me. We've been together for three years. Please, please, please." By this time I was on my knees by the front door. I wasn't embarrassed, and I didn't care what he thought. I needed William to say he would be with me.

"Leave me the fuck alone, you crazy bitch!!" He slammed the door in my face.

Why did he do this to me? He loved me, at least I thought he did. We had fun. I was beautiful to him. What am I going to do now? I can't breathe. My heart hurts. I got in my car, and I left. I was in shock. *I can't see the road, my tears are in the way. Maybe that's a good thing. I just want to run my car into anything to take away this pain I'm feeling. Are you listening? Again, you allowed someone to hurt me...I can't breathe. Oh God, noooooooo noooooo. I can't face tomorrow without him. I don't want to be by myself. Make him come back. Please make him come back to me.*

I wanted to run my car into every tree and every pole. I wanted to face death. Again. I cried so hard that I couldn't focus on the road. I held my chest because it felt as though my heart was coming out of it. The pain was intense. My tears were blinding me, but God took control of my steering wheel. And although there was no way for me to know it then, I knew I would someday live to have a man who truly loved and accepted me as his wife.

It wasn't long before I met Lee, my son's father, through mutual friends we were stationed with on Fort Campbell Army base. I knew I was in no shape to be in another relationship, but it didn't stop my desire to be loved He was very sweet and charming. I should have learned from our first date when he stood me up we weren't going to have a happy ending. Around that time, I was determined not to get hurt again so my guard was up for almost a week. *Right, not long at all.* He took me home to meet his family and that did it for me. He had a big family, seven sisters and four brothers. He also had lots of uncles, aunts, and cousins. I was in love at the fact that he had a family that I longed for all my life. Initially, visiting his family was rewarding. They lived in the country with very little entertainment. I don't think they had a working television until we began going home more often. There were all red clay roads through out the little town. His family lived in trailer homes scattered out on family owned acres. Although they didn't have much, they loved one another. I enjoyed late night bon fires and endless dancing to blues.

It wasn't long after Lee and I met we were married and my son was born. I don't wish to spend too much time talking about this relationship simply because it is pretty much like the others I had in the past except he made me an honest woman. I guess he loved me in the beginning but he wasn't in any shape to love only me; he loved women, and had his share of them.

We spent most of our marriage fighting. I was fighting for his love and he was fighting to remain single. During his infidelity, he had two children outside of our marriage, and I grew to love both of them dearly. In fact, after the second love child I had my tubes tied, because I believed we could be that "happy family." I believed that my husband would not cheat on my again. HA! You can't hate me for dreaming. I forgave Lee a long time ago. In spite of his actions he is a good person and we have a great friendship. Most of all, he gave me my angel.

On March 17, 2001, my life had already taken a dramatic change. That was the day I gave birth to my son, the day I became a mother.

To be honest, I was in denial when I first found out I was pregnant. I had been taking birth control pills up to a month prior to this discovery. I wanted to lose weight before I went to a particular military training, which I needed to get promoted to the next rank. Lee, my husband, had already been caught cheating numerous times, and financially we were struggling. I took a home pregnancy test and it was positive. I waited a few days and went to a clinic to take a blood test...and that was positive. I was very unhappy.

Don't get me wrong, I wanted a son. It's just that I knew I wasn't ready to take care of a baby, and I didn't have any idea of how to be a mother. I was afraid of failing at being a mother. I was also going through so much drama with Lee that I just couldn't enjoy being pregnant at all. So for countless days and nights I would cry to my friend who was very strong in her Christian faith and fifteen years my senior. I told her I didn't want a baby and maybe a third abortion was not such a bad idea. She said, "Baby, that baby is going to be a blessing in your life. You just hold on. God is going to provide all your needs and then some. You just watch. Don't let me ever hear you say anything about getting an abortion again, you hear me?"

I nodded yes, and all of a sudden I felt a burden was lifted off my shoulders. I fully accepted my pregnancy, and on that March day, after they cleaned up my newborn baby boy and placed him in my arms, oh my goodness, it was like I was holding a breath of fresh air! My son needed me, and I needed him. He was my angel, and to this day Angel is one of his nicknames.

When they took him away to be circumcised I felt as if I was going to have a panic attack. I needed to know what they were doing to him. One night in the hospital, I dozed off and he started crying. I begin crying and yelling at my husband for letting me over-sleep past his feeding time. The nurse came in my room wondering what all the yelling was about.

"My husband let me sleep past my baby's feeding time, now he is crying and hungry. I'm a bad mother. Twelve hours have passed and he hasn't eaten anything," I said frantically.

She smiled gently and said, "Baby, you didn't starve your baby. You were only asleep for thirty minutes. He's okay, trust me."

I picked up my baby and held him for hours. I let him sleep on my chest where I needed him to be.

Putting him in daycare was difficult for me because I didn't trust anyone to treat my baby the way I would treat him. I was very over-protective. I always worried about him, calling and checking on him throughout the day. If he was in a daycare I wasn't pleased with, I moved him to another one, but for the most part, God has provided him with good providers that I was able to eventually trust. He was such a lovable boy, which made it easy for providers to fall in love with him.

When my angel was only months old, I had to find a babysitter to watch him for almost 12 hours a day because my day started at 6 am in the military. While my angel was on the waiting list at child development center, I was referred to a family care provider who watched children out of her home for a large fee. Immediately, she rubbed me the wrong way. She wasted too much time bragging about the services she provided and how long she had been in the daycare business. Although I could see she was all about the money, I had no choice. I had to leave my angel with her. *Lord, please take care of our angel.*

In the beginning everything went smooth, I would drop by her home unannounced to make sure he was okay. As the weeks went by, my visits began to taper off and so did her caring for my angel. One day my unannounced visit didn't go so well. My Angel was sitting in the corner with a heavily soiled diaper. I literally lost my mind. I cursed her out calling her all sorts of words. She had the nerve to threaten to call the military police on me if I didn't leave.

I sat in the car crying holding my angel praying to God and apologizing to my Angel at the same time for not protecting him. My supervisor allowed me to stay home with until I found another sitter. I didn't need much time because I was next on the waiting list at the child development center. I never had a problem with a daycare provider since then, but my son spending the night with someone else was out of the question - period. I didn't even trust his father to be alone with him. Today I have gotten a lot better not only because my son is old enough to take care of himself, but because I learned that everyone is not out to hurt me and my son.

I adore my son, and although the teenage years are challenging, I'm prepared for the challenge. Some will say that my son is spoiled and I guess he is. He's spoiled but not rotten, and as far as I'm concerned he deserves all the love, attention and protection I can possibly give him. He's not just another child; he's the son of a woman who's been severely abused, verbally, mentally, sexually, and physically. Yes, every child needs to know and feel love, but my son, my angel, has been entrusted in *my* care—no one else's—and I have a responsibility and an obligation to love and nurture him, my angel.

When he was younger, people would tell me, "You baby him too much!" They just didn't understand my journey. My skin would crawl whenever anyone would discipline him, even though he might've done wrong. Every morning when I would drop him off at school, I worried that someone would tease him about his glasses or his stuttering.

I made it a point to not allow anyone else's opinions to persuade my decisions in raising my precious angel, but when I got married to Chris, he jumped in and changed a lot of things I had put in place. There were things I had suffered through in foster care that I wanted to make sure my son wouldn't have to deal with, like having a designated spot to eat in the house. Wherever I was, he was able to be with me and eat there. I hated the thought of him not only eating alone, but being alone. Period.

My Angel had a bassinet, a crib and a toddler bed, and he never spent one night in either of them; he slept with me up to the day my husband Chris and I married. I was sad when Chris insisted that my son shouldn't sleep in our bed anymore because I never wanted him to wonder if I had abandoned him. I had a very hard time leaving my angel in the room to sleep alone; it was almost traumatic for me. I'm so thankful that my husband was aware of my anxiety and instead of being demanding about the sleeping situation, he helped me to get through it. Today, I'm happy that Chris came in and broke up that bond because I didn't realize it was unhealthy. I was enabling my son, and I didn't even know it.

It's not easy for any woman to be a mother. I'm thankful my nurturing instincts surfaced on their own; it's easy for me to love my angel. Unfortunately, I have to mentally fight off those emotional triggers that want to whisper in my ear and take me back down my dark path of being abused. I am proud that I have not beaten, starved or degraded my angel. I broke the cycle. I am a loving mother.

My relationship with my father was distant and a constant roller coaster. Sometimes I loved him, but most days I didn't. When the military gave us time off, I was able to go to some of my father's family gatherings. I always felt out of place there, which caused me to leave earlier than everyone else. My family didn't understand why I was so distant with them. Truthfully, I wasn't trying to be distant. I was really trying to fit in, but it was hard. It was their mother, my grandmother, who ran the show. She was the one I couldn't stand to be around, but she was in control.

My two aunts would at least fake it, and act interested. They made a slight attempt to bond with me, whereas my two uncles treated me like family from the very beginning. They found some humor in my father having a love child. In their eyes my father was a momma's boy that couldn't do any wrong. Looking back, I can see that I was part of the problem. I was always angry at the fact that his mother knew about me and never said anything. And to make matters worse, she didn't feel any remorse for it either. It was evident that she didn't like me and I felt the same way about her. Sometimes she spoke to me and other times we would walk right past each other, our eyes faced forward. One time when we walked by one another, I tried to knock her ass down, but she moved out of my way quickly. *Bitch!*

When my father was around, everyone acted like they loved me and accused me of not receiving them. I would always have the same thoughts bouncing around in my head.

Get the fuck out of here! Are you listening to yourselves? Hello, I was neglected and abused for most of my life and you don't know why I hold some resentment? I was beaten, molested and talked down to all the way to the age of 17, while your little princess Patricia was being loved, nurtured and groomed for the world. You want me to do what? Get over it? You get the fuck over it! I'm sorry, I might be a little fucked up in the head and I'm making you feel a little uncomfortable. But to be honest with you, I don't give a red cent.

When my father's mother passed away, I went to her funeral, but only because it was my father's wish that I attend. I felt no sadness after hearing about her passing. I didn't feel anything. I couldn't even fake it. I walked up to the casket and stared at the white-headed woman.

Should I cry? Everyone else is crying. Personally I don't give a fuck about this funeral. I just had a D&C out-patient surgery on my ovaries a few days ago, and I am starting not to feel good. How did you manage to escape before apologizing to me? Did you ever love me? Why did you leave me out there like that? I guess I will never know, will I?

I walked away from the casket knowing that I would never get the answers I longed for. At the repast, I wrote her this letter on the back of her obituary.

I can't believe I drove this far to come see you dead. Hell, I didn't want to see you alive. Ain't this some shit, my stomach is killing me from this surgery and I'm up in here like I give a fuck. My daddy looks happy that I'm here though, which makes me feel a little better but not much.

Yeah, I looked down at you in there with pure hatred. For the first time you can't give back the same stare. I'm sorry you're in that pretty little casket...lifeless...but that's life. Everyone in here crying and I can't even crank out any crocodile tears. What!?!? Who in the hell are they talking about? Is this pastor talking about the same woman that left me in the streets to die with my mother? You knew damn well that my mother was pregnant by your son. It wasn't your decision to make for my father. She was 16 years old having sex with your 20 year old son. That sounds like statutory rape to me. What about you?

What hurts me so much is that you didn't even try to embrace me when I surfaced. Instead you fixed your mouth to say, "I knew about her but that was so long ago." I tried loving you. I really did. But you acted like you didn't do anything wrong. That's why my love turned to pure hatred.

I know you remember when Cynthia had a "family function" and you and I was walking down the same hallway in opposite directions. We didn't give one another eye contact but the tension between us was great in those few seconds. Neither one of us wanted to move over. And we didn't. We missed each other by a hair. If we did touch, you probably would have been in that box sooner.

Okay, right now I'm getting tight. I have my son here listening to this bullshit about how his great grandmother was this and that. He's still young so hopefully he will forget about this dreadful charade. Wrap this shit up. I need to go home and take my pain medication. Wow, look at your darling first grandbaby. She can't stop her tears from falling. Humph...

Okay, we're at the grave site. Everyone is saying their last goodbyes. Wow, they're gonna really miss you....Well, I'm glad this is finally over because now my pain is at 10. Finally, Bye! Won't be missed here.

Your bastard grandchild

Anger was already festering in my mind, my body and my spirit, but each time I thought about a time I was punched, kicked, denied food, neglected or called out by my name, a little more anger would find room to fester, and I welcomed it. After the anger, bitterness came and made itself at home in my heart. I entertained every unhealthy emotion that existed. I had reached a point of anger that I never experienced. No, I wasn't angry, I was mad. I was mad as hell. Mad at the people who abused me, mad at the people who knew I was being abused but didn't do a damn thing about it, and mad because I was chosen to go through this hell and there were other people out there who have never been hit, kicked, beat or called the ugliest of names.

So, what, is this my destiny? Did I deserve to live a life of hell? Was it my destiny to have a childhood of pain? Was it my destiny to have upsetting triggers that keep catapulting me right back into the hell I was trying to mentally escape from? Enough was enough. I was killing myself with the hatred that kept stirring inside me. I survived the horrific child abuse, yet I was killing myself because I couldn't handle being alive. I needed a cleansing and little did I know that having a family of my own would be the beginning of my cleansing process.

I was still legally married to my first husband when I met my current husband. We met at work. We were both in the same unit in the military. One morning he was helping me conduct a random urinalysis for our unit. After the eager bathroom goers gave their urine sample, Chris and I had a few more hours to wait for the rest of the testers.

I remember telling my friend who was also an assigned observer for the urinalysis that Chris was a very handsome man. She was like, "Girl, he is single, and he just sold his house in Virginia Beach, so he has some money." I'm not sure why, or how I found the nerve, but I was bold enough to ask my friend to give handsome Chris my phone number. We all were in the same unit; I worked in the administrative office and the two of them worked together as Basic Training instructors.

I anxiously waited for Chris to call, and he did. I was so happy. I can't remember our first phone conversation, but I do remember our first lunch date at Olive Garden. We enjoyed each other's company and started dating regularly, but my heart was still with my husband who had already transferred to Iraq. After a few months of dating Chris, I started to tear down the walls I had put up from day one. I could tell Chris was a good man; I knew it.

The simple acts of kindness that he displayed made me believe he truly cared for me. He also accepted my son, who was around 4 years old. We lived only five minutes walking distance apart. He had a three-bedroom house and I had a three-bedroom townhouse around the corner from him. On Saturdays, after he finished cutting his grass, he would walk around the corner with his equipment and cut my grass. After he cut my grass he would wash our trucks. This was his Saturday routine.

In the evening we would go out to wherever I wanted to go. He was and still is a perfect gentleman, opening doors for me (which I had never experienced before) and treating me on every date. He had exposed me to how a man should really treat a woman because I didn't have a clue. I was feeling something I had never felt from a man: love.

During this time, I realized that my ex-husband Lee was not the one for me and if I wanted to keep this good man, I would have to file for a divorce. And that's what I did. Lee did not want a divorce, but he was aware that I had moved on with my life. My finalization of my divorce decree was going to be mailed any day and I couldn't wait, because deep down inside I knew Chris wanted to make me his wife. He would make comments every now and then saying he bought me a ring, but I would play it off like I didn't believe him. Maybe I was still in denial about God sending me such a good man in my life. I wasn't used to good things happening to me. It was too good to be true.

One day, when we were having a small gathering at Chris's house, I said to him, "If you really brought me a ring, go and get it and let me see it." He chuckled and ran upstairs to get the ring. When he came downstairs, he said "here you go" with a smirk on his face. Right before I grabbed the beautiful brown Jared box, my best friend at the time said "no no, you better do it the right way," taking the box from both of us. She called my son, her children and her husband downstairs. "Okay, now you can properly ask my girl to marry you," she said with a huge smile on her face. To this day, I think Chris had some reservations about asking me to marry him at the time, because I was still legally married to my husband. But the divorce was moments from being final; I was just waiting on the paper work.

He got on one knee and asked, "Will you marry me" and opened the box to my one-carat diamond ring. I looked at my son and said, "What do you think sweetie?" At that time, everything in my life centered around my son. Period. If he wasn't happy, I wasn't happy. But I had already seen that he and Chris had their own special bond. "Say yes, mommy, say yes," he said, nodding his head in agreement. I said "yes", and six months later we were married.

I never thought I'd get here, but I consider myself to have the average family life. I could have ended up with another abusive man, but instead I'm married to a man who loves me and accepts me for who I am...most of the time. I know I brought more than my share of baggage into the marriage. I'm fully aware that I'm not the easiest person to live with. My issues became my husband's issues when we became one. I'm thankful for his patience and understanding. He was definitely chosen just for me. I like to think he was saved just for me.

I'm back in college, and this time I know it's the right time for me to continue my education. Someday I hope to be able to help girls and young women caught up in the kind of life I survived. Wow! I *really* would have never thought I'd get here. I survived! It's still not all perfect for me, nor do I ever expect it to be. I get depressed sometimes, and some days I still feel like I'm fighting against life. But it's different now. I have ME to rely on, and I've finally realized that I can *only* rely on ME for my happiness.

I'm still on my healing journey. I can't begin to describe everything that I've done to make it to this point. Truthfully, it makes me too tired and too sad to think of all I've done. The most important thing I do is take one day at a time, which helps the healing process to not seem so overwhelming or impossible. The best I can do is offer some random thoughts and a few letters that I have shared to help me keep going…and get here. I know some of my words may seem harsh, but sometimes when you've been beaten down and told how terrible you are for so many years, you have to sound a little rough to speak your mind and take back your soul.

Here are some of those random thoughts….

SLUT

I didn't sleep around because I was a slut. To be honest with you, I didn't even enjoy it. Never. I just wanted to feel wanted. Those men paid me some attention. I never thought that they just had one thing on their minds, which was to get what was between my legs and walk away. I honestly believed that every man I slept with really loved me.

I'm so ashamed to admit that I slept with over fifty men before I joined the military. I dodged every sexually transmitted disease, except for crabs. I got pregnant twice, just to have an abortion. I was trying to fill a hole that was too big to fill.

HYGIENE

I didn't learn proper personal hygiene until I joined the military. I didn't have the opportunity of my mother sharing her perfumes, body washes and favorite oils with me. I wore deodorant only from time to time—the cheap kind from Avon. It wasn't until I was in an open bay shower that I learned how to shave my underarms. My white battle buddies didn't look at me different because I had an armpit full of hair, though. They just instructed me on how to shave, with love. I think they felt sorry for me. If I never shaved my armpits, you know I never shaved my private area, or my legs. I also didn't know that as a lady, I should wipe going towards the back to prevent female infections.

I didn't start a daily routine of dental hygiene until I joined the military. I had braces when I was younger, but I picked them off because I didn't have anything else to do when I was lonely. Today, thank God, I have a pretty set of teeth. If you would look at me you would never know that I started from scratch learning what I should've learned as a child. It was rough. But I made it through.

THANKFUL

I need to be grateful that my mother carried me to term. I mean, she could've aborted me like I aborted my two. She could've beaten me to death in her stomach or smothered me to death when no one was looking. When she told me about that day I stopped breathing in the car on the way to the hospital, and how she hung my head out the window and I started breathing again, I always wondered if that was the truth or part of the truth. Did she try to kill me? Either way, it wasn't my time to go. And I am thankful. Really.

BUT IT STILL HASN'T BEEN EASY WITH HER

After I left my adopted family at the age of 17, I began to spend more time with my mother. Sometimes she loved me, sometimes she didn't. She could never put herself aside for me and love me. It's a different story with my baby sister Cheyenne. We are fifteen years apart and her will to survive is definitely a family trait. I first learned about my sister after I was adopted by the Black family, and that only gave Mrs. Black more ammunition to torment me. I just remember being so pissed off at my mother for having another child while I was being raised by these horrible people.

Although I was envious, I always loved my baby sister. She grew up into her own. My mother was so busy being in her own world that I don't know how she raised Cheyenne. But I believe between my mother's lovers and her AA/NA brothers and sisters, Cheyenne didn't lack love. Now she is raising my niece and nephew on her own, and I can't be more proud of her. She may not be making her money the corporate way, but I'm still proud of her hustle and determination to keep her children out of the "system."

Truth be told, I have still really loved my mother through most of my adult years. At least I tried over and over to love her, but she couldn't give the love that I deserve. In my opinion she is just like my grandmother. She looks and acts just like her. She resembles the very person that she hates so much.

I don't know why, but I was having a hard time one Mother's Day. I tried to reason with myself why I should call her and wish her happy Mother's Day. She didn't deserve it. Don't get me wrong, I forgive my mother for giving me up to the system. She did the best thing she could do at the time. Her upbringing was not all peaches and cream. She is a survivor and I am proud of her for that. It's just her actions in all these years that kill me. She is always depressed and angry at the world. I remember one letter she wrote to me:

———————————

Writing is very relaxing. I certainly encourage writing. I have cried my last cry. I have drank, done too many drugs, spent too much time in psych wards and carried 3 babies to full term, only to find out that I haven't a clue about mothering. My entire life has been a roller coaster of pain and suffering. I have lived a lifetime of being on the earth motherless and fatherless. I am and always will be bitter. It is a burning that is indescribable. I pretended that I never needed a mother or a father. I have spent a lifetime trying to be loved just because, only to realize that the breath in my body is as close as I will ever get to love. I am jealous of families, mothers, fathers and children. My eyes keep opening and once again the opportunity to breathe in and out the only real love I suspect I will ever know. Martha Ann and whoever the sperm donor is, did not and never did have my well being at heart. I care about my parents as much as they cared about me. It's sad that it hurt so bad that I keep these feelings in the shadows of my daily affairs.

mother

This is my reply to her letter

Diane,

I'm sorry to hear that you feel that way after all these years. When are you going to let that hatred towards your mother go, so we can move on?

After that dialogue with my mother, I wondered why I would give a fuck whether we would speak again or not. But on the next Mother's Day, I wanted to try. I couldn't find the nerve to call her, so I sent a text saying, "Happy Mother's Day 'Mother'...Enjoy your day."

"Same to ya," she texted back. I didn't expect anything more than that. Hell, I'm surprised that she responded. A few days later, I received an acceptance letter from the University of South Carolina's College of Social Work. I knew deep down that my mother was not going to respond to my text about my acceptance letter, but sometimes I do things to hurt myself. Especially with her.

After a few days of no response, I sent her another text saying, "My gut is telling me you have received my text, but I didn't expect you to be happy for me. You always called me slow and stupid behind my back. That's why I couldn't call you for Mother's Day. My circle doesn't know why I let you in my space. You don't deserve it. People don't want to be around you for a reason. Yeah, yeah, I get it…you're traumatized by your past…so am I. You need help!!!! If you don't change you're gonna die lonely, just like your mother did. It's scary, but you're just like her."

So I knew after this text that it would probably be a few years or never before we spoke again. How did I know that? Because that's how our generation curse works.

Epilogue

Dear Mrs. Black,

I know it's been a long time since we actually spoke with one another. When I left in 1991, I had no plans of coming back into your presence. I don't know if I will ever get the truth from you but I'll ask anyway. Why in the hell did you adopt me? Furthermore, why did you even take me into your house? You notice I said house and not home. I don't understand how foster parents like yourself continue to get kids and then they turn out to be worse than they were before they came into that house. You don't love them, so what is your motive? Money? I heard recently you had more foster children. What the fuck?!?!? What, that makes about 10 kids' lives you fucked up. You should be ashamed of yourself.

You treated Kelly, Robert and me like shit. For some reason, you treated me the worst, but it doesn't really matter. What was it? Was it because I was prettier than any of your crispy ass children? Was it my long beautiful hair? Did you see something in my eyes that told you that I was going to make it out from under your demonic claws? My God, and you had the nerve to go to church!

I am far from saying that I was perfect. To be quite honest with you I was fucked up. My mother left me, I just left my abusive grandmother, and I had no idea who my father was. What did you do? Sent me to the therapist and somehow or another I was labeled as "Mentally Retarded." You sneaky, conniving bitch. I wasn't "mentally retarded," I was emotionally detached. If I was mentally retarded I would have never accomplished the things that I have accomplished. Oh, wait, my bad, you got some extra money for that diagnosis. So instead of me being a crack head baby, nigga, stupid, goofy, bitch, a replica of my mother, I was actually your golden token.

I don't care how much you deny the mental and physical abuse that you have done to me. You know deep down what happened. Your physical abuse is forgotten. Hell, I will even forgive you for that. It's my heart and soul that you damaged with your negative name calling.

Where did all the money go that was given to you to take care of us? Why were your kids dressed in the finest and your foster kids were dressed like bums? Why did we have to eat rice and chicken every night while your kids ate whatever they wanted? You didn't teach me how to be a young lady. You didn't prepare me for the world that awaited me. I don't even remember you hugging me and telling me that you loved me. You just beat me until you got tired and called me names until I started to believe them myself.

I hope you are enjoying your homes that we bought for you. Everyone knew that we were getting mistreated, even your dysfunctional family. I get it. You didn't know any better. Right? You had it rough too in the sticks of Alabama as a child. Get out of here!!!!

You punished me just because you couldn't punish Rose, for whatever sick reason you came up with. You hated me!! You are fucking pathetic. I seen some recent pictures of you on Facebook and you look like death. You have no idea how what you did to me affected my life. It was rough but I made it through. You said I wouldn't be shit. I would be just like my crack head mother. Did you forget that your daughter was a crack head as well?

I feel sorry for Kelly and Robert. I feel bad for leaving them behind, but God gave me a way to escape and I ran. Their misfortune is because of your selfish greedy ass. We needed love and attention. Didn't they teach you that in your foster parenting class? Kelly has AIDS, sleeping with men looking for something that she should've got at your house. Robert is dead, due to your neglect. And where in the hell was Joseph? Robert, Terrance and Stanley needed a male role model.

Why did you get foster kids again? You don't have a loving bone in your body.

Well, Mrs. Pearlene Black, you will weep what you sow. Not my rules. However, if I had my way, I would tie your ass up and pour gasoline down your throat slowly until you gurgled the word "sorry."

PS: Tell your goons not to contact me because they feel like I disrespected you. Fuck you and Fuck them too!!!

- Truly your mentally retarded bastard child

A letter from Sheila

The Blacks' biological daughter- my older foster sister.

Hey Girl, I'm not going to curse you and use God in the same letter. Learn to do that if you don't want to continue to hinder your blessings. I need to lay something down on a line for you. First things first. Please talk to your real mother and her mother to find out why they cursed you and your future. Your blood line has nothing to do with us. Mr. and Mrs. Black were sent to you to save your life as a blessing because your real mother could have sold you for crack or some form of drug. Don't get it twisted. Sorry you so angry still. Why baby? It's not that serious that you chose to hold all this anger inside of you. Damn that was a long time, (by the way damn is not curse). Don't you know that could make you sick? Well anyway, a few more facts. As for a ice cream which you didn't get to enjoy, poor thing, it's ok because if your read about it today it was more healthy for you to have the ice pop, not the ice cream, get it. Also rice and chicken boo was healthier for you than McDonalds. You look like you have been so mad about it that you go there every day, just to make up for lost time. HAHAHAHA that was funny, have you read the news lately. Your letter made it seem that you had a personal talk with Satan, don't let him. You appeared to have been such a nice person, like everything was ok in your life, stop fronting with your little stuttering William and your gay lover on the DL. You know it runs in your family blood line. I am sorry that your mother did that to you. But you must also forgive her, she didn't know what she was doing also. It will all work itself out. If you don't want my prayers, then I will try not to include you in them, but really it's not up to me, God's got it. So the Blacks send their love to you for a peace of mind within. They don't need extra letters because they don't make sense and they were your saviors. Besides who cares and remember you are not in our lives anymore, we all moved on and grown girl. It's all your real mother's fault, talk to her and ask her why she did what she did and forgive her because Mr. and Mrs. Black have nothing to do with your curse. Check your ancestors. Ok I don't have a Facebook page because I don't want to be part of the web, but my children have one. So you will not see me on this stuff. If you want to send me a note, be nice and send it back to my daughter. Remember no cursing, because you are the only one angry. When you finish reading this note read the 23rd psalms and go to bed you're tired. Peace and love my ex sister.

Sheila

After all I've been through, I'm so thankful to be alive and well. Still, looking back over my life, it's hard to believe I survived all the abuse and neglect. Children are definitely resilient, and their ability to bounce back goes beyond an adult's imagination. Although resilience kept me, I still suffer from damaging thoughts that have the capability to destroy me physically and mentally.

Besides my own private thoughts, it amazes me that I haven't reacted to one of my abusers and delivered the same violent and vicious treatment to them that they've given me. I know I have to forgive in order to maintain an adequate level of peace of mind, but as I mentioned before, I've fostered damaging thoughts over the years, and these unwelcomed thoughts have the capability to not kill someone else, but to kill myself....

It was October 4, 2011, and I was working for the Army as a human resources specialist. At the time, I was really depressed. I didn't really have a close friend I felt comfortable talking to, so I would talk to my mother. I would talk to her almost every day, searching for something that would never be there with her. I so badly wanted her to love me and tell me that everything was going to be okay. Yes, I was 38 years old, but I had a late start.

On that particular day I was thinking about so much, yet not really thinking about anything at all, if that makes any sense. Life was happening all around me, and I couldn't figure out why it was happening the way it was. I seemed stuck in a confused and depressed state of mind. I had a bottle of pills lying in front of me, to ease some of my pain. I didn't want to kill myself, I just wanted to escape. That's when I called her, my mother, and it all started again.

"Hey, mother."

"Hey, what's up?"

"Nothing, I just feel really depressed. Depressed to the point of wanting to end it all."

"I hear ya, girl," she said, and the next twenty minutes was all about her and her issues. *Why do you keep putting yourself through the same thing with her? You know she will never be there for you, like you need her to be.* After those twenty minutes of her babbling about herself, I hung up the phone. I didn't even think about it twice, I just hung up.

I texted her a few moments later "privately"' through her Facebook account.

"Yes, Ma, I hung up the phone on you. You are never there for me. I always listen to you but you can't SHUT UP long enough for me to feel some motherly love. I know what you are going thru but DAMN!!!!"

Moments later, she posted this on my page:

"If you feel like you're not getting no mother love, go find it somewhere else. And if you want to jump…leap."

I posted back, privately:

"Really, on Facebook so that everyone can see? Did you just tell me to go "kill myself"? I sent you a personal message. Personally, I don't expect anything less from you. You're Sad…"throwingdownthemic"…LOVE and BLESSINGS!!"

Then I got this back:

"FUCK YOU AND EVERYTHING YOU LOVE!!!!"

Does she mean fuck my son, her grandson and my husband? Now she has crossed the line. I had to reply:

"YOU ARE A DUMB BITCH!! IS THIS SUPPOSE TO BE SOME KIND OF JOKE? YOU AINT SHIT AND WILL NEVER BE SHIT!! YOU FUCKING CUNT......YOU WILL NEVER BE ON MY LEVEL.

YOU AINT GOT SHIT AND WILL NEVER HAVE SHIT. SEE...I WAS TRYING

TO BE NICE AND LEAVE YOUR CRAZY ASS ALONE BUT YOU ARE STARTING TO CROSS THE LINE.

YOU WANT TO GO TO BATTLE WITH ME???? YOU WILL NEVER MAKE IT.....YOU FORGOT, IM YOUR BASTARD ASS CHILD AND I WILL GO TOE TO TOE WITH YOU. YOU THINK YOUR CRAZY, I'M CRAZIER......DUMB ASS, BROKE DOWN.....CUNT!!!"

Diane had a quick reply for that:

"HAHAHAHAHAHAHAHAHAHAHAHA LMAO LOL HAHAHAHAHA THANKS FOR THE ENTERTAINMENT FOR THE DAY... NOW GO BE ALL YOU CAN BE."

"GO TO HELL BITCH," I responded. And my mother was not done either.

"Glad to hear that you are having fun trying to hurt my feelings....too late you were born! Bulldog nice touch at least my man loves to touch me...unlike Chris who clearly wants to throw up at the sight of your big fat dufous ass....as for accomplishments hmmm you are broke pretending to live like the Jones' (stupid just your name is jones lmao), you are unemployable...in other words...just plain stupid...you are fat like a truck driver oh yea ran into your boy the other day and we had a laugh...you can hurt me with words and if you ever feel like you wanna some of my ugly ass bring it...so I can send you back to the only family that tolerates you in a box bitch."

Yeah, we had got caught in another fight, with words that really stung. Sometimes in the heat of the battle you say things you don't mean, but I knew deep down that mother really felt that way about me my whole life....

A few months later, I sent her an email trying to break the vicious cycle that we have been subjected to for all our lives together.

December 25, 2011

Good Morning, I hope all is well.

I would like to make peace between us. Your mother fought with her mother and now we are fighting with each other. WE made a vow that we would break this vicious cycle, and I would like to live up to that vow. We cannot take back what we said to one another but we CAN move forward. We may not like one another but I love you. We may not be able to rebuild our relationship, but we can love each other from the distance.

I love you, mother…let's not block our blessings.

Your daughter
    Shandreka Monic' Jones

I didn't receive a response, but I wasn't expecting one either. I guess I just got to keep moving forward. And remember who I am. I am a Butterfly.

She Was Me

Before I met her, all I heard from all directions were negative things about her.

"She's angry all the time," he said.

"She fights in school," she said.

"She was moved countless times to group homes and foster homes because of her bad behavior," he said.

"If she doesn't get her way she will act out," they all said.

Wow, she has some issues. Why do they want me on this case again?

"Has anyone taken the time to hear 'her' story?" I asked. "In between foster homes and group homes has anyone stuck by her side, letting her know that they are there for her, no matter what? Better yet, since everyone has something negative to say about her, has anyone spent one day in her shoes? Or did you just do your job, file your negative report, send the child on her way and never look back?"

"I'm pretty sure that if anyone took the time to see what this child sees we won't be fixating on the negatives, but praising her positives," I continued.

I have to be honest. I was afraid to meet her, although I am the best person for her. I am the only one who can look at her and say, "Wow, you are so adorable. You are just beautiful. How can anyone treat you so bad? I understand that you don't trust anyone. I know your caseworkers, your foster parents, your group homes, your grandparents, and your mother and father have all failed you. But now I'm here…"

I finally get the nerve to tell her, "I know you don't know me, but you can trust me. I will never hurt you. I am here to save you."

The pain in her eyes is unbearable. But there is no turning back now because…she is me.

Little Monique

Monique in the United States Army

Stages of Life

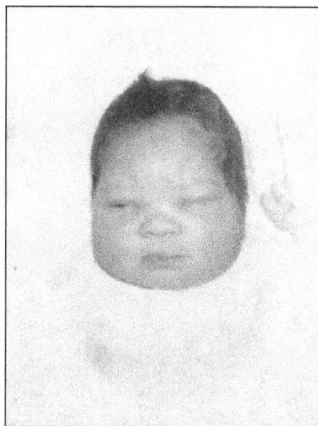

Monique and Uncle Gerald

Monique and grandma

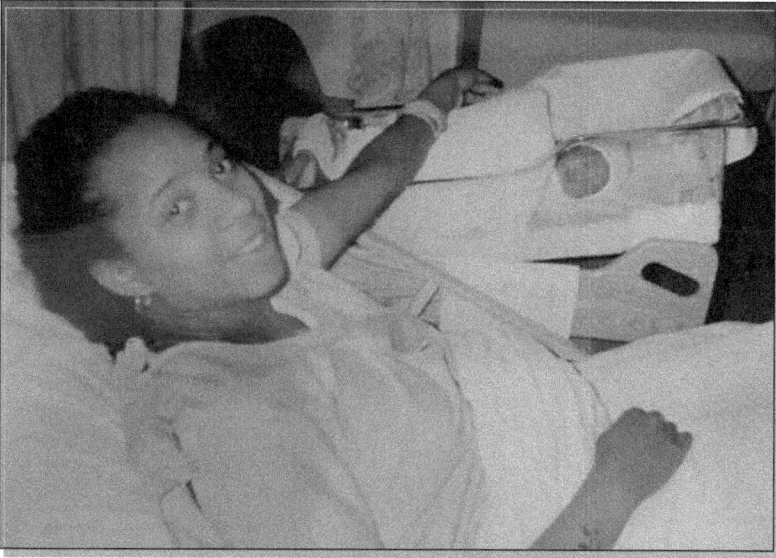

I thank God, the generational curse of abuse was not passed on to me. When my angel was born, I loved him unconditionally, and I always will.

Monique and son

**My husband, Chris, a man who loves me beyond the baggage
in my past and with a promising love for the future.**

My birth mommy as a little girl.

I often wonder what my life would have been like if this little girl, my mommy, pictured above had received the love and attention she deserved as a child. Abused by the hands of her own mother, she later had a daughter of her own, me. I believe my mother wanted to love and nurture me, yet she wasn't given the tools to know how to love; she wasn't loved herself. She did what she knew to do. I'll always love my mommy.

There are so many children around the nation in need of a home. Being a foster parent is a rewarding experience, whether for several days or several months. If you feel you can't financially afford to take a child in, there are plenty of resources available for you and the child.

After experiencing and sharing so much of my pain, I wondered if things would ever change with the foster care system. Things had to change, but how? When? What's the solution of something that seems to be an epidemic?

I believe providing services to the birth family could possibly result in alleviating the root of the problem of the high need for foster homes. The child welfare policy is a good policy that is in place to protect vulnerable children, however, I think the policy can use a few modifications to put more emphasis on helping birth families.

To strengthen the services provided by child welfare agencies, partnering with community-based organizations and providing individualized support and services to birth families would be a good start. Based on my research, many children who are placed in foster care originate from families who have very limited resources and multiple problems.

Many of these families are poor. They live in rural areas and are often simultaneously coping with substance abuse, physical illness, mental illness and/or domestic violence. These services are available, but child welfare does not openly offer the services offered to these families. In many cases, children who are removed from their homes do not receive a follow up action plan. Meanwhile, the child is being moved from one foster home to another while oftentimes being mistreated and abused.

In many cases, some birth families are unknowledgeable of what is required to properly care for their children. In those cases children should be removed from their home and placed in a safe, loving environment. As stated earlier, children are not always placed in a safe, loving foster home. There are many cases where children are being mistreated while they are in foster care.

My second recommendation is for child welfare services to add more tailored support and services to foster parents and to ensure that child welfare workers are adequately trained. I do not believe that foster parents are properly recruited or given adequate training. According to the Foster Care Licensure manual, foster parent applicants are only required to participate in a minimum of fourteen hours of training prior to initial licensure, which, in my opinion, is not enough training.

I believe if the child welfare policy was modified to help birth families better care for their children, family reunification will increase and the need for foster homes will decrease; however, we have to cease the abuse in foster care simply because we need to protect our children. Many families open their homes and heart to vulnerable children who've been removed from abusive and neglectful families, yet foster families are seldom fully informed about what the child has been through.

Foster parenting is by far, one of the hardest duties that anyone can assume. Not only does the foster parent have to provide a safe environment for the child, they must also work with child welfare agencies, schools and other outside agencies to ensure the child's needs are meet. There are foster families who genuinely care about the needs of children who've been taken away from their family. However, the responsibility can be overwhelming and they will either stop foster parenting or they will allow the child to fall through the cracks of the system by only collecting their check and neglecting the needs of the child. Research proves that foster parents struggle with getting proper support from Department of Social Services case management, which results in the child being further neglected.

In order to rectify this problem, child welfare agencies must provide foster families with acute case management support. They must lengthen the required hours for the initial training to allow more time to thoroughly discuss the challenges of foster parenting and the resources available. My recommendation will be to develop more support for foster parents and make sure that the child welfare system is trained to respond to the foster families needs.

I am completely aware that my recommendations would take time – a lot of time, but there is a solution to every issue, and this issue is one requiring immediate attention. Foster care children continue to be abused and as long as we simply discuss the issue and collect statistics, the problem will remain.

I can only do my part in my small corner of the world, and that is to be a voice for children who have been abused and are still being abused in foster care homes. I thank God for those foster care parents who've taken on the task and understand the importance of giving children a loving, safe environment to live in. It's not easy at all, but thank you for your love. Every child deserves to experience a loving home, caring parents, and a bed to sleep in at night – preferably not alone in a cold attic.

Now You Know

An estimated 679,000 children were victims of abuse and neglect (unique instances).

47 states reported approximately 3.1 million children received preventative services from Child Protective Services agencies in the United States.

Children in the first year of their life had the highest rate of victimization of 23.1 per 1,000 children in the national population of the same age.

Of the children who experienced maltreatment or abuse, nearly 80% suffered neglect; 18% suffered physical abuse; and 9% suffered sexual abuse.

Just under 80% of reported child fatalities as a result of abuse and neglect were caused by one or more of the child victim's parents.

(www.nationalchildrensalliance.org/cac-statistics)

CHILDREN'S RIGHTS is proving that failing child welfare systems not only can be fixed but can be made to run well…
(www.childrensrights.org)

The Annie E. Casey Foundation and Jim Casey Youth Opportunities Initiative is an organization that focuses on transforming the child welfare systems, reforming the juvenile system and tracking child wellbeing.

Their vision is for every young person leaving foster to have the opportunities and support needed for a successful transition to adulthood.

In any given state, there are hundreds of young people at risk for leaving foster care without permanent connections to a stable family and community. Each year, 23,000 young people transition without the typical growing-up experiences that teach self-sufficiency skills, and without the family supports and community networks that help them make successful transitions to adulthood. As a result, these young people experience very poor outcomes at a much higher rate than the general population:

- More than one in five will become homeless after age 18
- Only 58 percent will graduate high school by age 19 (compared to 87 percent of all 19 year olds)
- 71 percent of young women are pregnant by 21, facing higher rates of unemployment, criminal conviction, public assistance, and involvement in the child welfare system
- At the age of 24, only half are employed
- Fewer than 3 percent will earn a college degree by age 25 (compare to 28 percent of all 25 year olds
- One in four will be involved in the justice system within two years of leaving the foster care system

Nationwide, they help bridge a gap in services for these young people so they can have the opportunity to achieve a better path as they transition from foster care to adulthood. (**www.aecf.org**)

Court Appointed Special Advocates (CASA) for Children, is a network of 949 community-based programs that recruit, train and support citizen-volunteers to advocate for the best interests of abused and neglected children in courtrooms and communities. Volunteer advocates—empowered directly by the courts—offer judges the critical information they need to ensure that each child's rights and needs are being attended to while in foster care. (casaforchildren.org)

- Children with CASA volunteers get more help while in the system...and are more likely to have a consistent, responsible adult presence.
- Children with CASA volunteers spend less time in foster care and are less likely to be bounced home to home.
- CASA volunteers improve representation of children.
- Reduce the time needed by lawyers
- More likely than paid lawyers to file written reports
- For each of 9 duties, judges rated CASA/GAL volunteers more highly than attorneys
- Highly effective in having their recommendations adopted by the court
- Children with CASA volunteers do better in school
- Less likely to have poor conduct in school
- Less likely to be expelled
- Neighborhood resources, interested adults, sense of acceptance, controls against deviant behavior, models of

conventional behavior, positive attitude towards the future, valuing achievement, ability to work with others and ability to work out conflicts. (CASA for Children.org)

Foster Care to Success is among many non-profit organizations providing tuition grants as well as book money, living stipends and emergency funding for the unexpected expenses that could derail the most dedicated student on a tight budget. They also provide academic coaches, personal mentors, care packages and internship opportunities to the 5,000 young people we serve annually, enabling them to enjoy a college completion rate many times that of their peers who lack such support. **(fc2success.org)**

ACKNOWLEDGEMENTS

My brothers and sisters - I want you to know you are not alone and it is never too late to find peace and happiness! I know this to be true....I am walking this path!

My younger foster sister who is a product of abandonment and abuse - My heart aches for you. I pray you find peace and happiness soon. To my foster brother, may you continue to rest in peace.

Both of my foster parents - I have exceeded your expectations and then some. I carried hatred in my heart for many years...I forgive you.

To my mother - Thank you for putting aside your pain, so I could share mine. Thank you for carrying me in your womb for nine months, protecting me and not going to an abortion clinic when all odds were against you. I love you for giving me life. You are my hero.

To my son, my angel - I love you more than life.

To my husband - Thank you for saving me. Thank you for showing me unconditional love to my angel and me. Thank you for your continuous support while I wrote his book. I love you!

Judy Figura, LCSW – For pushing me closer towards healing by helping me learn more about myself.

Kevin Quirk – For helping me get started on my book writing journey.

To all my friends, near and far, who supported me during this journey - You know who you are. I thank you and I love you!

Candy Publishing, LLC

www.candypublishing.net

Candy Publishing is an independent publishing company designed to help aspiring writers put their life in print. We work on-on-one with writers to create eye-catching, one-of-a-kind memorable books. Each book is a personal experience.

We bring your book to life.

Butterfly in the Attic
www.abutterflyintheattic.com

Cover Art
Deborah Shedrick
www.dshedrick.com

Editing
Dr. Sandra Winborne

DK1 Promotions
www.dk1pro.com

SmartPR Consulting, LLC
www.smartprconsulting.com

www.ingramcontent.com/pod-product-compliance
Lightning Source LLC
LaVergne TN
LVHW051519080426
835509LV00017B/2101